Walk
in Her
Sandals

D0096953

"This book truly makes the scriptural account of Christ's passion come alive! Readers will find themselves entering into the story in a whole new way and experiencing the unique gifts and central role of women. A treasure for spiritual growth during Lent and Easter!"

Mary Healy
Associate professor of Sacred Scripture
Sacred Heart Major Seminary

"You'll find yourself walking as a companion to Jesus and toward Easter in a whole new way, thanks to the treasure within this book."

Sarah Reinhard
Catholic writer, blogger, author, and editor of *Word by Word*

"*Walk in Her Sandals* is a devotional tapestry, richly woven from the poignant threads of women's intimate experiences of Jesus. Experience how those moments forever changed their lives, and moment by intimate moment, you, too, will be changed."

Sonja Corbitt
Catholic speaker, radio host, and author of *Unleashed*

"Kelly Wahlquist's stunning team effort, *Walk in Her Sandals*, dramatically raises the bar for women's resources with its innovative approach to exploring feminine gifts as pathways to Christ."

Lisa Mladinich
Catholic author and creator of *Amazing Catechists*

"In *Walk in Her Sandals* you will hear a symphony of wisdom, insight, and practical application. What this team of women has accomplished is remarkable. They have opened up a world of opportunity for other women to enjoy their relationship with God and at the same time discover aspects of their being in a new and profound way."

Jeff Cavins
Founder of *The Great Adventure* Catholic Bible Study Program

"*Walk in Her Sandals* teaches readers to use imaginative prayer by bringing to life the women who accompanied Christ through his passion, death, and resurrection. It seeks to help contemporary women discover their own call to be missionary disciples in the service of the New Evangelization. Many will benefit from reading this book."

Most Rev. Andrew Cozzens
Auxiliary Bishop of St. Paul and Minneapolis

Walk in Her Sandals

Experiencing
Christ's
Passion through the
Eyes of Women

Edited by **Kelly M. Wahlquist**

Founder of WINE (Women In the New Evangelization)

AVE MARIA PRESS AVE Notre Dame, Indiana

The Catholic Edition of the *Revised Standard Version* of the Bible, copyright 1965, 1966 by the Division of Christian Education of the National Council of the Churches of Christ in the United States of America. Used by permission. All rights reserved.

© 2016 by Kelly M. Wahlquist

All rights reserved. No part of this book may be used or reproduced in any manner ritten permission from Ave Maria Press®, Inc., P.O. Box 428, Notre Dame, IN 46556, 1-800-282-1865.

Founded in 1865, Ave Maria Press is a ministry of the United States Province of Holy Cross.

www.avemariapress.com

Paperback: ISBN-13 978-1-59471-691-1

E-book: ISBN-13 978-1-59471-692-8

Cover image © stocksy.com, thinkstock.com.

Cover and text design by Katherine Robinson.

Printed and bound in the United States of America.

Library of Congress Cataloging-in-Publication Data

Names: Wahlquist, Kelly M., editor.
Title: Walk in her sandals : experiencing Christ's passion through the eyes of women / edited by Kelly M. Wahlquist.
Description: Notre Dame, Indiana : Ave Maria Press, 2016. | Includes bibliographical references.
Identifiers: LCCN 2016017368 (print) | LCCN 2016031878 (ebook) | ISBN 9781594716911 | ISBN 1594716919 | ISBN 9781594716928 () | ISBN 1594716927 ()
Subjects: LCSH: Jesus Christ--Passion--Meditations. | Catholic women--Religious life.
Classification: LCC BT431.3 .W35 2016 (print) | LCC BT431.3 (ebook) | DDC 242/.643--dc23
LC record available at https://lccn.loc.gov/2016017368

Contents

Introduction

In my prayer that crisp autumn morning, as the sun glistened on the brightly colored leaves that had fallen on my deck, it was as if Jesus was lovingly looking into my soul and gently pleading with me.

"I need you," he said.

I didn't let the Lord finish what he had to say. "What does that mean, Lord?"

The silence was deafening. It was as if the Lord was preparing my heart to hear something of grave importance.

"I'm listening," I told God.

Closing my eyes, I pictured Jesus before me.

"My body is battered, bruised, and broken, and I need you—as women—working in the beautiful gifts you've been given in your womanhood, to heal me," Jesus said.

Immediately my thoughts turned to St. Francis. Just as the Lord said to St. Francis, "Rebuild my Church," in the recesses of my heart on this October day, I heard the Lord saying to me and to women everywhere, "Heal my Body."

There is no doubt that in the world today, the Church, the Mystical Body of Christ, is being repeatedly assaulted. We need only turn on the television, open a newspaper, or surf the Internet, and instantly we see how our Lord continues to be persecuted. It can be disheartening at times, but as followers of Christ we do not lose heart. Our hope is in the Lord.

For the last twelve years I have ministered to many faith-filled women, traveling the country and connecting with others just like me—people on fire to share the Gospel and make Jesus Christ known and loved. I have encountered women from every walk of life: mothers, nurses, lawyers, teachers, bank tellers, psychologists, writers, bus drivers, artists, and pastoral leaders. Their lives were marked with irrepressible

sensitivity, compassion, and generosity. Their hearts were
focused on bringing others to Christ to be healed. Now, it was
as if Christ was calling them together to be part of a greater
healing.

As the faces of my women friends and colleagues sur-
faced in my memory, the Lord's words echoed in my ears:
"I need women to work in the beautiful gifts they have been
given as women and to heal my Body."

So many of these dear women were purpose filled, driven
by an insatiable desire to serve their Lord. Their maternal
instincts and innate sensitivity to others could be used, pow-
erfully, in the kingdom of God.

It was a moment of profound illumination. This was a
divine summons, a call that could not be ignored. The Body
of Christ needed more than just a Band-Aid. It needed to be
healed.

But who could lead this charge?

God has bestowed upon all women graces that allow
us to understand and to enter fully into our mission as his
disciples. He has gifted us with receptivity, sensitivity, generosity, and intuitive maternal gifts, all of which allow us to
know our heavenly Father on a deeper, more intimate level.
St. John Paul II in his letter to women, *Mulieris Dignitatem*,
said, "Christ speaks to women about the things of God, and
they understand them; there is a true resonance of mind and
heart, a response of faith."

*Okay, Lord, you've captured my mind and heart. Where do I
begin?*

That autumn day in 2012 is now just a distant memory.
But I took the Lord's words to heart. After talking with some
of the wisest women I know, we decided to pool our gifts
and write a collection of Lenten reflections by women and
for women. That's how the book you are now holding came
to be. It is our hope that as you enter more fully into Holy
Week as a woman, you will enter more fully into the paschal

mystery and be continually transformed into the woman God created you to be.

How to Use This Book

Walk in Her Sandals: Experiencing Christ's Passion through the Eyes of Women allows you to enter more fully into Jesus' passion, death, and resurrection in a new and profound way—as a woman living the beauty of your giftedness. The structure of each chapter is purposeful. We begin with "A Moment to Ponder" as we set the stage for the theme of that chapter and prepare you to embark on the journey that awaits you that day.

Next, "Enter the Scripture" provides the riches of the readings of sacred scripture that correspond with that day, both in the biblical narrative and in the liturgical year. Reading the scripture citations provided beforehand makes for a powerful experience.

Following the scripture reading, "Walk in Her Sandals," a fictional narrative, draws you into the story and allows you to experience what it may have been like for women who lived and walked with Jesus. Like so many modern-day Catholic women, these ancient women were seekers and sharers of healing.

Next, in "Unwrap the Gift," a specific gift related to womanhood is explained so that you begin to understand anew the beauty of your dignity and vocation as a woman—you embrace your *feminine genius*.

Having entered the scriptures, walked in the sandals of a woman during the time of Jesus, and unwrapped your gift, you will be guided to "Reflect on the Meaning" by one of your sisters in Christ who is striving for holiness just like you. These practical stories offer insight, encouragement, and inspiration for you on this journey.

You'll continue your reflection with "Lectio." Here you will be led in *lectio divina* (a prayerful reading of sacred scripture), provided to draw you deeper into an intimate relationship with Jesus.

Since we know that as Catholics we live, learn, and worship in community, and since we know that as women we are "radically relational," we have added "Questions for Group Discussion" to each chapter. One of the best ways to use this book is in the small-group setting with other women. In fact, we at WINE: Women In the New Evangelization created this book for that exact purpose. If you are interested in learning more about the national women's ministry WINE: Women In the New Evangelization, visit www.CatholicVineyard.com and be sure to check out the information provided on the last page of this book.

The final section of each chapter, "Walking in the New Evangelization," will help you to use your gifts to bring others to Christ. This section offers two ways to contribute to the New Evangelization: first, by growing in your contemplative spiritual life; and second, by giving you practical suggestions to enhance your active spiritual life.

To assist you as you walk through the various aspects of each chapter and encounter the unique and beautiful styles of the individual writers, I have provided a few comments or suggestions. These interjections are italicized and serve to weave the many pieces together seamlessly.

As you read the selected scriptures, enter into the narrative, and ponder these reflections, you might find yourself asking, *How am I being called to be a disciple like the women in the Bible? In what ways can I heal the bruised and battered Body of Christ?*

This Lent, I'll be praying for you, my sister in Christ. May this book trigger a grand conversion in your heart. May these stories draw you into the passion, death, and resurrection of Jesus in a new and profound way, and may your heart be softened (evermore) and your ears be opened.

Perhaps you will hear the Lord speak to you as he spoke to me. Maybe you'll hear him say,

My dear one . . . heal my Body.

Does this seem like too big a challenge, too great a task? If we try to do it on our own power, we would undoubtedly fail. To inspire you to take up this journey with confidence, my friend Pat Gohn starts us off by reflecting on a passage from the eleventh chapter of John's gospel, in which we meet two of Jesus' closest women friends: Mary and Martha, who had just lost their beloved brother, Lazarus.

Believe and See the Glory of God

by Pat Gohn

In the weeks leading up to his passion, death, and resurrection, there's a powerful moment in the lives of Jesus and his dear friends at Bethany, where the Lord and his followers would often visit as they went to and from Jerusalem. Jesus' in teaching this moment of truth stands as an important watchword for this book and our examination of Holy Week and Eastertide.

The gospel recounts Jesus' raising of Lazarus, Martha and Mary's dear brother and a good friend of Jesus (see Jn 11:1–54). Lazarus died before Jesus arrives, and his friend has been in the tomb for four days. Curiously, Jesus had heard his friend was ill yet failed to hasten to his friend's bedside. Now, by all appearances, it was too late to do anything but try to comfort the mourning sisters.

And in fact, when Jesus arrives Martha and Mary are encouraged by his presence. Martha openly trusts in Jesus when he predicts that her brother will rise again, as he declares to her, "I am the resurrection."

Martha's faith is emboldened. She calls Jesus the Messiah, "the Christ, the Son of God!" Yet even faith-filled Martha protests Jesus' next move, when Jesus asks that the stone before the tomb be removed. "Lord, already there is a stench" (Jn 11:39).

Yet hear these challenging and inviting words from Jesus:
"Did I not tell you that if you would believe you would see
the glory of God?" (Jn 11:40).

After that, Jesus prays, and the dead man, Lazarus, is
raised. A miracle!

It was to be Jesus' last public miracle, for it set in motion
the Pharisees' nefarious plan to put Jesus to death.

Let us thoughtfully consider these words of Jesus as we
begin this book. Let us be on the lookout for the glory of God
in these weeks of praying with the paschal mystery of Jesus'
passion, death, and resurrection.

If *you* would believe, *you* would see the glory of God. I
once read a beautiful expression of this: "Something of the
glory of God shines on the face of every person."[1]

Just stop and think of that—the glory of God is on *your
face*, good woman!

How is this possible? It is possible because the God of creation made you in his image! "So God created man in his own
image, in the image of God he created him; male and female
he created them" (Gn 1:27). This means that a woman who
fully lives her dignity as a woman gives glory to God! In other
words, something of the *genius* of God is in you! God's image
is reflected in the genius of humanity's creation. Women and
men reflect God, in some important ways, in who they are as
human persons. That's fantastic!

Within the dignity of the human person we discover
another theme that we're going to explore more in this book:
the genius, or the gift, of womanhood. (Yes, of course, there
is a complementary masculine gift, but that's not this book.
This book is for women.)

When it comes to celebrating the beautiful dignity and
vocation of womanhood, women have a friend in St. John
Paul II who described it as the *feminine genius*. (How do you
like that? You're a *genius*!) John Paul II's pontificate offered
teaching documents and homilies that extolled women and
dignified their feminine gifts. In this book, we're going to

explore four gifts that are naturally and spiritually inherent in women: receptivity, generosity, sensitivity, and maternity. We're also going to examine the two gifts of faith that increase the graces we need in our lives: the gift of prayer and the gift of the Holy Spirit.

We'll delve more deeply into these gifts as we go along. While we can reflect upon our feminine gifts at any time, the scriptures are particularly rich in their exploration of our sisters in faith in the gospels—in particular, in the final week of the life of Christ. For this reason, we are focusing on the events during Holy Week and Pentecost, when we see the glory of God expressed in a most extraordinary way. Something of the amazing relationship that Jesus Christ has with us is on display during this part of the liturgical calendar. Something of the glory of God is found in contemplating Jesus as he walks toward Calvary and beyond.

No matter what time of the year you find yourself pondering this revelation, it is something momentous; it is not to be missed. As we reflect on this season of grace through the lens of our womanly gifts, may we come to understand, truly, that something of the glory of God shines in us!

So let us walk with Jesus so that our faith and our giftedness may grow. And may we believe and see the glory of God!

1.

The Gift of Receptivity

(Palm Sunday)

A Moment to Ponder

by Kelly Wahlquist

In the fifth century BC, the prophet Zechariah records the words of the oracle who foresaw the Messiah who would restore God's kingdom:

> Rejoice greatly, O daughter of Zion!
>   Shout aloud, O daughter of Jerusalem!
> Lo, your king comes to you;
>   triumphant and victorious is he,
> humble and riding on an ass,
>   on a colt the foal of an ass.
> I will cut off the chariot from E'phraim
>   and the war horse from Jerusalem;
> and the battle bow shall be cut off,
>   and he shall command peace to the nations;
> his dominion shall be from sea to sea,
>   and from the River to the ends of the earth. (Zec 9:9–10)

After Jesus fulfills this prophecy in the final week of his life (see Mt 21), the promised Messiah goes on to reveal himself first as the Suffering Servant, then as the Lamb of God who takes away the sins of the world, and finally as the King of Glory. In obedience to his Father and for love of us, our Savior wholeheartedly embraced his role in the fulfillment of God's salvific plan.

Thirty-three years after the great mystery of the Incarnation, he set the stage for an even greater mystery. In this final week of his passion, death, and resurrection, our Lord showed us what it means truly to abandon ourselves to love.

This total abandonment, within the feminine genius, reveals itself in the feminine gift of *receptivity*, the feminine charism that is at the heart of this chapter. As we examine the significant events in the final week of the life of Christ and beyond, we will see how each of these affected those closest to Jesus and how understanding these events can deepen our own relationship with God as we follow him with increasing faith, hope, and love.

If we are willing to open ourselves to what God has in store for us, we will see in a fresh way the transforming beauty of the Cross, whether with the anticipation of waving palms or the hindsight of resurrected glory. And as we see that beauty, may it give us courage to take up the little crosses of our lives and follow him.

Enter the Scripture
by Sarah Christmyer

In this chapter we will be delving into the passages of scripture most commonly associated with Jesus' final triumphant entry into Jerusalem (Mt 21:1–9; Mk 11:1–11; Lk 19:28–40; Jn 12:12–19).

The week before Pope Francis came to the United States for the World Meeting of Families, all Philadelphia was buzzing. I've never seen anything like it. Everyone—Catholics, Protestants, Jews, and "nones"—was talking. "Are you going?" "Did you get tickets?" "You must be excited!" Skeptics thought it was all hype, that people would flee the crowds. Others agonized over how to get into town. "I can't believe so many roads will be closed," was a common complaint. "Who is this guy?" a neighbor asked me. "They don't do this even for the president!"

More than once, I was reminded of the week before the first Easter, the day Jesus entered Jerusalem. "Who is this Jesus?" is the question everyone was asking. They'd heard of his miracles. Some were skeptical: had he truly raised Lazarus from the dead? Others were simply cautious. His disciples, the Jews, and the Romans had been watching him for weeks. Now he was headed from safety in the northern region of Galilee, down to Jerusalem where the Jewish leaders wanted his head.

Jerusalem was abuzz with preparations for Passover. Jews came from the four corners of the earth to attend the festival, and Jerusalem and the surrounding towns were bursting with pilgrims who were already in a festive mood when they heard that Jesus was coming. And so, "a great crowd who had come to the feast" gathered palm branches and "went out to meet [him]" (Jn 12:12–13). As people "spread their garments" on the road ahead (Lk 19:36), the "whole multitude of disciples" who were walking with him "began to rejoice and praise God with a loud voice for all the mighty works that they had seen" (Lk 19:37).

The Pharisees tell Jesus to rebuke the crowds, but it's no use. "If these were silent, the very stones would cry out" (Lk 19:40). Yes, even the stoniest hearts melted that day; the scriptures tell us that "all the city was stirred" by this explosion of praise and joy as Jesus enters Jerusalem (Mt 21:10). "Stirred" is an understatement. The same Greek word is used in Revelation 6 when a great earthquake sends the stars tumbling to the ground like figs from a tree in a gale. This country boy is rocking the big city.

Before this, Jesus often told people not to talk about him or call him king. Now he plays right into their expectations. He sends two disciples into the village to get a young donkey they would find tied up there.[1] You and I might think he's tired, but those around him know better. Without a word, the disciples do as he asks; they fling their cloaks on the donkey and help him onto it. As he rides into Jerusalem, Jesus is acting like a king at his coronation.

What did that look like? The Old Testament gives us an idea:

- **1 Kings 1:32–46** tells how King David, when he calls for Solomon to be anointed king after him, has him ride to his anointing on the king's own mule. Not coincidentally, the people rejoice until the city is "in an uproar" (v. 45); "the earth was split by their noise" (v. 40) Matthew alludes to this when he describes Jesus riding a mule into Jerusalem.

- **Zechariah 9:9** prophesies the return of the Messiah[2] like this: "Rejoice! . . . Lo, your king comes to you; triumphant and victorious is he, humble and riding on an ass, on a colt the foal of an ass" (in some translations, "donkey"). We might expect a king to ride a white charger, a war horse. But the prophet portrays the king riding humbly on a donkey, bringing peace.

- The people around Jesus get the picture, as they did in the Old Testament. In **2 Kings 9:13**, people threw their garments on the ground for King Jehu to stand on while they proclaimed him king. The prophets told them what to expect, and now the crowds around Jesus are seeing it. No wonder they throw down their cloaks and cry, "Blessed is the King who comes in the name of the Lord! Peace in heaven and glory in the highest!" They are quoting Psalm 118:26, an enthronement psalm. The long-awaited king is being received by his people as he enters the holy city.

As we wave palm branches at the start of Mass on Palm Sunday, we too are welcoming our King. I'm always startled when we move from waving palms to a reading of the entire Passion narrative. In the Church calendar, Palm Sunday is also Passion

Sunday. We all read it together, as two people read the parts of narrator and Christ, and then we take the part of the crowd as they shout, "Crucify him!" It makes you realize that the same crowds who call him king soon call for his death. And in a cosmic irony, it's the crucifixion that vaults Jesus to his throne, making him the king they had hoped for—but in a way they could never have imagined.

Triumph joins with death in another way as well. The palms we wave at the beginning of mass are later burned and then blessed for use the next Ash Wednesday. They remind us even as we rejoice in Jesus' coming that he died for our sins.

Hosanna! Blessed is the king who comes in the name of the Lord! Are we willing to receive a king who comes "in ashes"? Can we receive a king who looks not like a king at all but like a piece of broken bread, or a person who is poor, sick, or needy? Who is this Jesus, our King? How do we receive him?

Walk in Her Sandals: Anah's Story

by Stephanie Landsem

Anah hurried toward Jerusalem's upper market, wondering why the streets were so quiet the week before Passover. No pilgrims thronged the streets to gape at Herod's enormous palace or stare at the Temple soaring higher than the city walls. Perhaps she'd be able to make her purchase quickly. She found the potter's stall but no potter sitting beside his wares. She browsed through the clay jars; surely he'd be here soon.

Her thoughts went to the preparations she needed to make this week: wheat and wine, and the lamb must be chosen and brought to the Temple. Jerusalem would be crowded for the feast, especially if what she'd heard about Jesus was true. He'd be here for Passover, and the Sanhedrin would be watching him. Unease prickled over her skin. For her mother's sake, she prayed they were just rumors.

Close by, the cry of a newborn babe made Anah's heart skip a beat.

"Shh." A woman about Anah's age—perhaps twenty years—stood among the vessels with an infant in her arms and a little girl beside her. The baby quieted, but the girl pulled at a jar, almost toppling it on her head. Anah caught it just in time.

"Forgive me," the mother took the little girl's hand and pulled her away from the pottery. "I shouldn't have come here with these two. You're fortunate to be able to go to the market by yourself."

Anah forced her lips into what she hoped was an understanding smile as the mother shooed the child down the street, but the familiar pain pierced her heart. She didn't feel fortunate. She felt empty.

For five years, she'd prayed for a child to fill her womb, to bless her as it seemed every wife in Jerusalem had been blessed. She'd lain awake at night, asking the Most High how she had sinned against him, but no answer came. She was empty and hollow, just like the jar in her hands. When would the Lord hear her prayers? When would her life have a purpose?

Carefully, she set the jar in its place. *How long, O Lord, will I wait for your answer?*

Anah did her best to be faithful. She took care of her husband—and everyone else in her household. She was a good wife, a good daughter-in-law, but not a mother.

In the street, a boy dashed past. She called out, motioning to the empty stall, "Where is everyone?"

"Jesus, the Nazorean," he answered, his voice breathless. "They've gone to see him."

Anah's heart dropped to her stomach. So the rumors were true. "Where is he?"

He shouted over his shoulder, "The Sheep's Gate."

Anah hesitated, her thoughts tumbling. Jesus. Back in Jerusalem. The man her mother and her brother, James, followed. The man all of Jerusalem had talked about, who had—if the talk at the well could be believed—raised Lazarus of Bethany from the dead. The man who had angered the most powerful men in the city.

The last time Jesus had come to Jerusalem, there'd been threats of arrest, and Jesus had stayed with a secret disciple. Anah hadn't even seen her mother or James. This time, Ephraim said the Pharisees were determined to arrest Jesus—and his followers. If she could find her mother and James now—today—she could bring them home. She could keep them safe.

Anah rushed down a winding back street and around the wood market. Soon, she heard the sound of a crowd, like the rumble of thunder. She stepped out of the dim street into the harsh sunlight. The open square around the Sheep's Gate teemed with people. Her heart pounded, and her mouth dried with the dust stirred by the crowd. Please, let them not all be here to see Jesus. If only he'd slipped into the city quietly, unnoticed. It would have been so much safer, for everyone.

Beside her, a man lifted a small boy to his shoulders. The boy pointed, "He's coming!"

Anah dodged elbows and stepped on feet as she pushed her way to the front. She must find her mother now, or it would be too late.

Suddenly, she emerged at the gate and her mouth fell open in disbelief. Jesus. But not walking into Jerusalem as a poor traveler from the country. No, he rode in on a white colt. Following him and surrounding him were pilgrims—hundreds of them. They shouted and sang, waving palm branches in the air. Some took off their cloaks and threw them down in front of Jesus.

What was he thinking? The chief priests were looking for him, and he marched into the city as if he were the new David, returning to claim his kingdom!

The pilgrims shouted as they passed by, "Blessed is he who comes in the name of the Lord!"

"Peace in heaven and glory in the highest!"

All around her, questions flew like sharp stones. "Who does he think he is?"

"Who declared this man king?"

A shiver of fear skimmed over Anah. Everyone knew the prophets words: "Do not be afraid, daughter Zion, see your king is coming, seated on a donkey's colt." These pilgrims thought they were seeing the fulfillment of the prophecy.

Anah glimpsed the familiar faces of Jesus' disciples among the throng. There! Her mother, and close beside her walked James, tall with a bushy beard. Both of them were smiling.

"Mother! James!" She waved her arm high and stepped out into the street. In an instant, her mother's arms were around her.

"Anah, can you believe it?" She motioned to the crowded street. "Listen to them."

Anah nodded as she stood back to inspect her mother. Time and travel had etched new lines around her eyes, but they were bright with excitement. Miriam was her mother's name, but Anah knew Jesus and his disciples fondly called her "the other Mary."

"Sister," James caught her in a hug like a scruffy bear.

Anah raised her voice to be heard over the crowd, "James, we must talk—the Pharisees, Ephraim says—"

But James turned away, distracted, as three well-dressed Pharisees pushed to the front of the crowd, and at the same time one of the disciples—was that John?—shouted out, "Blessed is the king of Israel, who comes in the name of the Lord."

One of the Pharisees stepped to block Jesus, his face like thunder: "Teacher, rebuke your disciples."

Jesus stopped the donkey. His face was calm, but his voice cut through the noise of the crowd: "I tell you, if they keep quiet, the stones themselves will cry out."

Anah gasped. The Pharisee's eyes narrowed, and his face darkened. Two disciples—tall men with broad shoulders—stepped closer to Jesus, towering over the Pharisee with grim faces. The Pharisees stepped back, and the crowd surged forward, pushing Jesus along with them.

"James," Anah turned to her brother and said firmly. "It's not safe." Especially if Jesus was going to talk to the most powerful men in the city like that. "Come home with me."

"I must stay with Jesus." He wore the fierce expression she knew well.

She pressed him. "At least have Mother come. She looks tired."

James let out an annoyed breath but nodded.

Miriam opened her mouth to object, but Anah knew just what to say. "Joses would like to see you."

Miriam frowned, and Anah knew she'd prevailed. Joses was Miriam's oldest child, and when she'd left more than a year ago to follow Jesus, he had been hurt and angry. Anah and Joses had always been close. Until now. She had watched in sorrow as Joses's anger had turned to bitterness, as he had closed himself off from her and even from Veronica, his young wife.

James turned to their mother. "Let Anah take care of you for a few days. I'll tell Mary; she'll understand."

Miriam gave in. "Send word as soon as you know where you'll stay. I'll come."

The crowd was loosening as Anah took her mother's arm, weaving through the scattered groups until they were on the winding street leading into the center of the city, answering her mother's many questions. "Yes. Ephraim is well. Grandmother is anxious to see you." She breathed a sigh of relief as they reached their own neighborhood.

Miriam stopped and put her hand on Anah's arm. "And you, Anah? Are you . . . ?"

Anah pressed her lips together and shook her head. Her mother's hopeful eyes clouded, but she squeezed Anah's hand. "The Lord's will be done. He has a plan and a purpose for you."

Anah turned away. "Let's not talk of it now." The Lord may indeed have a plan for her, but why did it not include children, the one desire of her heart? What was her purpose if not to be a mother?

At the gate to their courtyard, Miriam stopped. "Is Joses here?"

Anah shook her head. Her brother, a scribe at the Temple, would come home when evening fell, and he'd have plenty to say to their mother.

"Is he still angry with me?"

Anah frowned. "You know how he is. He doesn't understand why you left." In that way, she agreed with Joses. Her mother had left everything—her daughter and a newly married son, a grandchild, and her own aging mother—to follow after a man no one, not even James, could explain. As a widow, it certainly wasn't unseemly for Miriam to follow her youngest son, but what did she and James see in Jesus that the rest of them did not?

"When he hears about Jesus, he'll change his mind."

Joses change his mind? The Temple would fall before her stubborn brother would change his mind, but she didn't need to remind her mother of that. She unlatched the gate and pushed through the door. There would be plenty of time to talk about Joses, now that her mother was where she belonged.

They entered the gate to a modest-sized courtyard flanked on two sides by sturdy clay houses. Two families lived here, as was common in the crowded city. The larger of the two houses belonged to Joses. The other was where Anah and Ephraim lived with Huldah, Ephraim's widowed mother. A fig tree gave its shade, and roses climbed the high wall. In one corner, the coals of a cooking fire glowed, and in the other a small garden showed sprouts of green.

"Miriam." A young woman with a child in her arms rushed forward. Joses's wife, Veronica, was dark haired and graceful with a tranquil smile and eyes as sparkling as the night sky.

"Veronica . . . and can this be Benjamin? Oh, how he's grown!" Miriam threw her arms around them.

A stout middle-aged woman came out of a dim doorway, wiping her hands on a cloth, her hearty face creased in joy. "My dear friend," she snatched up Miriam's hands. "I've missed you."

Miriam kissed her friend's cheek. "Huldah. I've missed you too. You've been taking good care of Anah."

Huldah harrumphed and patted her daughter-in-law affectionately. "She takes care of us all, like a mother hen. I hardly have a thing to do."

Anah smiled, but a sorrow pricked her like a needle. She knew Huldah meant it kindly, but she didn't need reminding that she was a mother with no children. Surely, her mother-in-law was disappointed in her but too good-hearted to let it show.

"Let me see my daughter, will you?" came a trembling voice. Anah's grandmother, Zilpah, made slow progress across the courtyard. She had come to live with Joses after James and Miriam had left to follow Jesus. Zilpah stopped in front of Miriam and scrutinized her with eyes as bright as glass beads. Miriam took her frail mother in her arms and kissed her parchment cheek.

"Have you found the Messiah?" Zilpah asked, her mouth and her voice quivering with age. "Have you found him, my girl?"

"I have, Mama." Miriam said, her voice full of joy. "I have found him. I will tell you all he has done, and you will know he is the one we've been waiting for."

Anah felt the familiar unease. Was her mother right, or had she been taken in by a fraud, as the Pharisees and scribes—even Joses—claimed? She turned away to hide her doubt. "First, you must rest."

Veronica, Huldah, and Zilpah brought Miriam into the shade of the fig. Anah poured water in a wide bowl and added a sprig of lavender, but worry coiled in her chest. Just because Jesus rode a white colt into Jerusalem like the new David didn't mean he was the Messiah. There had been plenty of imposters before. And what about the danger from the Pharisees?

". . . cured the sick, even lepers," her mother was saying as Anah brought the water. "And in Bethany . . ." She turned wondering eyes on Anah. "You know them, Anah—Martha and Mary of Bethany. Their brother, Lazarus, had been dead— in the tomb!—for four days."

Anah sat beside her mother. She'd heard it at the well but hadn't believed it. And Joses had outright scoffed. Her mother surely didn't lie, but how could such a story be true?

"He really raised a dead man?" Veronica breathed, her eyes alight with wonder.

"Yes," Miriam answered. "And so much more I can tell you."

"But what about the Sanhedrin?" Huldah voiced Anah's thoughts. "They say they want him arrested—"

"And the things he says," Anah interrupted. Joses said he blasphemed. He forgave sins and called himself the son of the Most High. She didn't want to be like Joses, but perhaps her brother was right. A shiver of foreboding chilled her. Something terrible was going to happen—to Jesus, to his followers, and maybe even to her mother and her brother.

Her mother regarded her with understanding, as if she knew her thoughts, her sudden fear. "Don't listen to Joses. Listen to Jesus." Miriam took Anah's hand in hers. "Keep your heart open, Anah. He says, 'All that have ears to hear, listen to me.' Listen, my daughter, with your ears and hear with your heart."

Anah looked over the gathered women. Zilpah smiled toothlessly. Huldah knitted her brow in concern but seemed ready to listen. Veronica's eyes strayed to the gate, no doubt worried Joses would come home early. And her mother—she looked sure and peaceful and full of purpose.

She still wondered about Jesus—and worried over her mother and brother. But she would listen—if that's what her mother asked of her.

She was ready. "I'm listening, Mother; tell me about Jesus."

Unwrap the Gift of Receptivity
by Pat Gohn

This adaptation of the Palm Sunday story is especially beautiful because of the wonderful ways in which the womanly gift of receptivity are played out in the lives of these characters, particularly the childless Anah, who remains open to the plan God has for her, even though that plan takes a different form from the one she had envisioned. Can you relate to this? Most women can, which brings us to this week's feminine gift! —Kelly Wahlquist

Receptivity is a powerful, positive womanly gift. If you associate the word "receive" with "receptivity," you are on the right track. Receptivity offers a strong foundation for the other womanly gifts we'll talk about in the chapters that follow.

The basics of receptivity can be easily seen biologically. A woman's body is made to receive others, is designed for intimate relationships and openness with others. Within marriage, for example, a wife can receive the love of a husband in a physical way. She is capable of conceiving and nurturing a child within her body, and nourishing it after its birth. Receptivity, therefore, is part of a woman's human nature. While not all women will be married or will give birth to children, *all* women have the gift of receptivity, simply because they are women!

Biology is just one aspect of receptivity; it is also a spiritual and emotional gift. A woman is receptive to others when she draws another close to her heart. How naturally women do this in response to love! Receptivity is a life-giving response to another. It is relational. It says yes to another's existence, receiving him or her for who he or she is.

The ultimate example we have for receptivity is our Blessed Mother, Mary. At the moment of her *fiat*—her "let it be to me" at the annunciation—Mary said yes to God the Father's invitation to love, to become the Mother of Jesus (see Lk 1:26–39). Her yes invited the overshadowing of the Holy Spirit whereby she was filled with the glory and love of God and conceived Jesus in her womb.

Receptivity says yes to love. It's a yes to God's plan. Mary did not hold anything back from God. In return, God does not hold anything back with Mary. She is, therefore, a conduit of many graces.

Mary allowed God to do great things in her. May our receptivity imitate Mary's openness to God's plan unfolding in our own lives. As we consider receptivity in light of Palm Sunday, we envision Jesus riding on a colt triumphantly into Jerusalem. The people are praising him! What a reception!

Imagine the women in that crowd who were blessed by Jesus' words and deeds over the years. Their receptive response to him reflects how Jesus first treated them.

"Jesus treated women with openness, respect, acceptance and tenderness. In this way he honored the dignity which women have always possessed according to God's plan and his love" (John Paul II, *Letter to Women*).

Your receptivity can have a positive impact in God's plan for the world. As you come to Palm Sunday, consider your gift of receptivity:

- As you make preparations for the family celebrations and events of Easter, how are you preparing to receive Jesus as your King and Savior, and to let him do great things in and through you?

- Each time you go to Mass, how do you prepare yourself to receive Jesus in your heart when you receive the Eucharist? Afterward, how do you nurture that spiritual life within you and enter more deeply into relationship with the Lord so you can better understand his plan for your life?

- How do you nurture the souls God sends into your care so that they may grow closer to Christ and his Church? What is one thing you can do to help them grow in their love for God this week?

Reflect on the Meaning: Palm Sunday

by Lisa Hendey

I live in a yard that's sprinkled with a dozen palm trees in a variety of hybrids. My husband lovingly planted each of them during different phases of our lives, punctuating the landscape adorned with an orange tree, my Mary garden, the boys' old tree house, and our new drought-tolerant landscaping. Looking at the palms in their various shapes and sizes brings a smile to my face. Each of them tells its own story about our lives in this place we've called home for more than fifteen years.

Greg's love for palm trees is as much a part of his personality as is his classic-rock guitar hobby, his training as an ER doctor, or the vintage VW bus we drive to Mass each Sunday. My Indiana native–born spouse associates palm trees with California. And I associate palms with him. So palm trees make both of us happy.

Perhaps it is not surprising then that I look forward to Palm Sunday every year. In our parish home, our RCIA elect and candidates mark the occasion in a special way by waving large ten-foot palm fronds during the opening procession at our morning Mass. During this annual liturgical tradition, my husband now plays his guitar with our choir. And I sit in the pew, watch the procession, and listen to the opening hymn; I give thanks to God for this man who has drawn me so deeply into my faith in such unexpected ways.

More than a decade ago, Greg was one of those palm-waving RCIA candidates. On that particular Palm Sunday, I sat in the pew with my two young sons and cried happy tears at the prospect that my beloved husband would soon join us at the Eucharistic table when he received his sacraments less than a week later at the Easter Vigil. While I myself am a cradle Catholic, journeying with Greg into the Church reignited in me a passion for Jesus Christ that was new and surprising.

I'd "believed" in the faith given to me by my parents since birth, but somehow praying for my husband's journey toward Christ had resulted in a new kind of receptivity toward God in my own life, my own powerful conversion. When Greg finally joined us to receive the precious Body and Blood on that much-anticipated Holy Saturday night, I somehow discovered for myself—perhaps more profoundly than ever before in my life—the true presence of Jesus Christ in the Eucharist.

In praying that we might be united in the Eucharist, I found my own powerful yes to God's will for my life. I now realize that while I was praying for Greg's spiritual journey, God was carrying me along my own path to his loving arms, using my vocation as a wife and mother to draw me more deeply into my own relationship with Jesus Christ as a partner in the domestic church of our home. And so, while I continue to pray lovingly for my sons and husband to know and love God in their lives, I also never take for granted my own spiritual receptivity.

These many years later, I now find Palm Sunday to be both a joy and a challenge. As we gather at church to receive our blessed palms and hold them aloft, it's easy to unite myself mentally with the throngs who lined that road into Jerusalem and shouted "Hosanna!" as they welcomed a king into their midst. I would have been there with them, my cloak spread across the road in recognition of the Master. "Hosanna!" I would have shouted, loudly blessing the name of the one who came in the Lord. Swept up in the excitement, it would have felt easy to believe.

But the challenge of Palm Sunday washes over me as soon as our Liturgy of the Word turns to the Gospel proclamation of the Lord's passion. So quickly, we have forgotten our "Hosanna!" affirmations. Like Peter, even in my professed belief, I have too often denied Jesus in word or deed. I am now with the crowd, jeering "Crucify him!" My tears overflow onto the palm frond in my hand as I recognize that my own sins pound those nails into Christ's hands and feet. "He came to die for me," I remind myself, "that I might have a chance at eternal life." I kneel in silence as the gospel passage announces that the Messiah has breathed his last. And then I am alongside the centurion, nodding as he proclaims, "Truly this man was the Son of God!" I am one of the women who followed him to Jerusalem, mourning his loss and waiting fearfully for the unknown.

Somehow, the majesty and the passion of our Palm Sunday liturgy never grows old in my heart. We know through scripture and divine revelation the path to salvation that will unfold as we journey toward our Easter Alleluias. But draped in the violet of those waning days of Lent, we must each assess for ourselves the yes we give to Christ's place in our hearts. On Palm Sunday, as I process forward to receive him in Holy Communion, the weight of this amazing miracle often exceeds my capacity for gratitude.

My "Amen," so simple and yet fully heartfelt, is my yes.

Yes to loving you by better loving my family.

Yes, even in the midst of doubt, pain, or struggle.

Yes, not because of what others will think, but because of the truth of who you are in my life.

Yes to loving you by being your hands and feet to a world so greatly in need, because this is what you have called me to.

Hosanna, Lord. Save me. I give myself fully to you.
Yes, Lord, I am yours.

*Palm Sunday can elicit all kinds of responses, depending on your
situation. Perhaps in years past you've been so preoccupied with
keeping the kids from poking each other in the eye with palm fronds,
or keeping them quiet through the long gospel reading, you've found
it hard to put yourself in the scene and imagine how you would have
responded had you been there, witnessing firsthand the events at
the Sheep's Gate.*

*God knows this. He waits patiently for you, ready to meet you
where you are. While the events of the Passion are rooted in history,
the significance of each moment transcends time. Take a moment
now to put yourself in that time and place, there beside the Blessed
Mother as she watches her Son pass through the gate.* —Kelly
Wahlquist

Lectio for Palm Sunday

Read John 12:12–19, and read it a second time more slowly.
Then read it for a third time, noting the words or thoughts
that jump out at you.

> The next day a great crowd who had come to the feast
> heard that Jesus was coming to Jerusalem. So they took
> branches of palm trees and went out to meet him, crying,
> "Hosanna! Blessed is he who comes in the name of the
> Lord, even the King of Israel!" And Jesus found a young
> ass and sat upon it; as it is written,
>
> > "Fear not, daughter of Zion;
> > behold, your king is coming,
> > sitting on an ass's colt!"
>
> His disciples did not understand this at first; but when
> Jesus was glorified, then they remembered that this had
> been written of him and had been done to him. The
> crowd that had been with him when he called Lazarus

out of the tomb and raised him from the dead bore witness. The reason why the crowd went to meet him was that they heard he had done this sign. The Pharisees then said to one another, "You see that you can do nothing; look, the world has gone after him." (Jn 12:12–19)

Now, ask yourself:

- What do I hear? (Write down the words or phrases that stand out to you as you read.)

- What does it mean? (Write down what you think about those words, or why you think they're important.)

- What is Jesus saying to me? (Write what you hear Jesus saying into your heart, and respond to him.)

Questions for Group Discussion
by Dr. Carol Younger

1. *Enter the Scripture.* We see so many clashing images in the Palm Sunday liturgy: joyful shouts, palms waving, and then the Passion. "Hosanna" and then "Crucify him." A triumphant procession of the King and then a humiliating death on the Cross. Life is filled with contrasts. Joy in suffering is one of those contradictions. When we experience suffering, we don't always see the beauty and joy that will come after or through that suffering. In what past experiences can you now see beauty, or even joy, coming from suffering?

2. *Walk in Her Sandals.* At the beginning, Anah is as empty as the jar she wants to purchase. That void is filled by fear, disappointment, and the need to "mother" others. Counseled by her mother, Miriam, to tune out the comments of others and to listen to Jesus, Anah settles in beside her mother, turning toward the hope that peace and purpose will fill her receptivity. What fears or disappointments

do you tell Jesus when you pour out your heart? In what way has he taken even just *one* of those, shown you his purpose in it, and given you peace?

3. *Unwrap the Gift.* Another name for receptivity is "emptiness." Unless one is empty, there is no place to put the gift. Where in your life do you feel empty? What desires of your heart have not been fulfilled? What might God's purpose be in those desires? What might God be preparing you to receive in the "shape" of that emptiness? (For example, infertility may lead a woman to give her time and energy to supporting other mothers, or to other pro-life activities.)

4. *Reflect on the Meaning.* While Lisa prays for Greg's spiritual journey, God carries her along in *her* path. When have you prayed for someone else and found an answer *you needed for yourself*? Our need for Jesus to carry us prompts in us the same response as Lisa's: *Yes, Lord, I am yours.* Share your prayer experience for others and the gifts to you that flowed from those prayers.

Walking in the New Evangelization
by Kelly Wahlquist

As we conclude this chapter, think about what new insights or "God prompts" you have experienced as you reflected on the experiences of these women. Here are a couple of ways you can continue to reflect upon what you have discovered in the coming week!

Contemplate Your Own Gifts

The Passion narrative says, "Fear not, daughter of Zion; behold, your king is coming, sitting on an ass's colt!" (Jn 12:15). How often do we let fear hinder our joy? God does not want his children to fall back into fear but to rejoice as coheirs with Christ—to suffer with Christ, so that we may be glorified with him (see Rom 8:14–17). Prepare to enter into the Passion of Jesus in a new and intimate way. Sit quietly for five minutes as you begin your day, slowly breathing in and out, and with each breath say to Jesus, "Lord, I abandon myself to your love." Let perfect love cast out all fear as you begin this journey.

Faith in Action

On that first Palm Sunday, as Jesus rode into Jerusalem on a colt, everyone stopped what he or she was doing to catch a glimpse of him. How blessed we are to know that the King of kings is present among us today and that we too can serve our King by continuing his work on earth.

1. Take time out of your busy schedule to be in his real presence. Even if it's just for a few minutes, with kids in tow, try to stop by your church for Eucharistic adoration this week.

2. Remember the cloaks thrown on the ground before Jesus as he entered Jerusalem? Take the time to go through a closet and find some clothing to donate, and then to deliver it to a charity near you.

2.

The Gift of Generosity

(Holy Thursday)

A Moment to Ponder

by Kelly Wahlquist

If you ever make a pilgrimage to the Holy City, be sure the "Cenacle" is on your list of places to visit. This is the Upper Room where Jesus celebrated that last Passover with his disciples. It is here he washed their feet and where he first celebrated the Eucharist; and, fifty days later, it is where the promised Paraclete first descended upon the men and women at Pentecost, leaping overhead like tongues of fire.

It all began with a simple request: "Go into the city to a certain one, and say to him, 'The Teacher says, My time is at hand; I will keep the Passover at your house with my disciples'" (Mt 26:18). And so they did. Two thousand years later, we remember Jesus' breathtaking gestures of generosity and love on that holy night.

What generous act is the Lord asking of you today? Are you ready to greet him in the Cenacle of your heart?

Enter the Scripture
by Sarah Christmyer

In this chapter we will take a look at the events associated with Holy Thursday: the institution of the Eucharist at the Passover celebration, described in the synoptic gospels (Mt 26, Mk 14, and Lk 22), and the foot washing prior to the Passover celebration, described in John 13.

The day Jesus entered Jerusalem, every man, woman, and child in Israel and beyond had been anticipating the Passover for weeks, as certainly as most of us start Christmas preparations right after Thanksgiving! For weeks in advance the shops announced it, music filled the air, houses were made ready, and the markets teemed with people ordering food for the feast.

It was the month of Nisan, circa AD 33, and hundreds of thousands of people were converging on Jerusalem for the week-long feast of Passover. One of three great pilgrim feasts, Passover (*Pesach* in Hebrew, for "passing over") commemorates the liberation of the Hebrew people from Egypt and the establishment of the nation of Israel. Every Jewish male, wherever he lived, was required to make the trip to Jerusalem at least once in his life for the feast. Jews who lived closer would attempt to go every year.

On the tenth of Nisan, an enormous flock of lambs raised specifically for the occasion was led from nearby fields into the city. Only lambs without blemish were allowed for the sacrifice, so for three days they would be painstakingly examined. Those passing muster were led to the slaughter, to be offered on the altar and consumed at the Passover meal, which recalled God's command to the Hebrew slaves to sprinkle the blood of lambs on the doorposts of their homes, as a sign for the angel of death to "pass over" their homes and spare the lives of their firstborn sons (see Ex 12).

Jesus' last week in Jerusalem echoed the fate of those Passover lambs. God's firstborn son would not be "passed over" but would willingly lay down his life for all. Jesus entered Jerusalem, was examined for three days by the Jewish leaders, was tried by the Roman authorities, and when no fault was found in him, was chosen for slaughter (see Jn 19:6–7).

Not even those closest to Jesus suspected what was in store that week Jesus entered Jerusalem and was hailed as a king. "His hour" had come (Jn 13:1)—the fulfillment of his mission on earth. They did not realize he wasn't in Jerusalem to celebrate Passover in the way the other pilgrims were there. Jesus went to Jerusalem for Passover in order to transform the central feast of the Jewish faith into that which all Passovers, since the first one, pointed to: freedom from sin and the power of death, to be the children of God.

All this was lost on the Twelve, who simply wanted to celebrate the Passover with Jesus. And so, on the fourteenth of Nisan, the day lambs were sacrificed, Jesus sent Peter and John to prepare the feast in "a large upper room" that had been made ready for them (Lk 22:7–14).[1]

The Passover Seder was structured around the pouring and blessing of four cups of wine, including a "cup of blessing" poured and shared after the meal was consumed. It also involved blessings, prayers, and the ritual washing of hands before each course. The first or "appetizer" course included lettuce or parsley that the participants dipped in a kind of salad dressing before eating it. A variety of foods were served for the main meal along with unleavened bread and the meat of the sacrifice.

Everything done and said at a Seder was prescribed, and everyone knew the ritual. As Jesus said the blessing over the bread at the main course, imagine the astonishment of the Twelve as he added, "This is my body which is given for you" (Lk 22:19). (Imagine what the disciples must have thought the first time they heard this. "*What* did he say? His *body*?") Then after supper, they would expect the cup of blessing—but Jesus

added, "This cup which is poured out for you is the new covenant in my blood" (Lk 22:20). What could it possibly mean?

Think of how jolting it is for us today when even one
word of the Mass is said out of place. Not only was he changing the words, but also what he said was electrifying. The old
covenant between God and Israel, which was sealed with
blood on Mount Sinai, had been broken ages ago. But God
had promised to make a new one: "But this is the covenant
which I will make with the house of Israel after those days,
says the LORD, . . . I will put my law within them, and I will
write it upon their hearts; and I will be their God, and they
shall be my people. . . . I will forgive their iniquity, and I will
remember their sin no more" (Jer 31:33–34).

That day is here, and the new covenant will be made in
Christ's blood! It is Jesus' self-offering at the Passover that
turns his execution into a sacrifice. Jesus identifies himself
with the sacrificial lamb. He makes *himself* food and drink for
the new covenant family.

The synoptic gospels don't tell us what the apostles
thought of the Lord's declaration. John, who tells us in chapter 6 that they determined to accept the "hard saying" that
we must eat his flesh and drink his blood to have eternal life,
focuses on something else Jesus did after the Passover meal.

During supper Jesus rose and "laid aside his garments."
He clad himself in a towel, poured water, and washed the disciples' feet. Washing feet was the job of a household slave, not
a rabbi. This was a major statement. Jesus inserted it into the
Passover to make a point. His greatness is born out of humility
and self-giving. His kingship is born of self-offering. The way
he lays down his garments and takes them up again (see Jn
13:4, 12) foreshadows the way he will willingly lay down his
life—and take it up again.[2]

Matthew and Mark tell us that after singing a hymn,
Jesus and the disciples went out to the Mount of Olives (see
Mt 26:30; Mk 14:26). Very likely that hymn was Psalm 118
or Psalm 136.[3] Both praise the Lord for his steadfast love.

Psalm 118 is a psalm of victory. "The stone which the builders rejected has become the head of the corner," it proclaims. "This is the day which the Lord has made; let us rejoice and be glad in it" (vv. 22, 24). How appropriate for Jesus to be singing this as he heads to the Cross!

The Lord is preparing his disciples to see in his death a victory. He is also preparing them to love. As they head out into the night, he tells them they cannot follow where he is going. "A new commandment I give to you, that you love one another; even as I have loved you, that you also love one another" (Jn 13:34). Later, he tells them, "Greater love has no man than this, that a man lay down his life for his friends" (Jn 15:13).

Holy Thursday marks the end of Lent and the start of the Easter Triduum. At midnight, the day of the Lord's passion will begin. As Mass ends, we hear, "Stay with me, remain here with me, watch and pray, watch and pray." The lights are dimmed, and the Eucharist is removed to the altar of repose. The altar is stripped, and crosses are covered. There will be no Mass until Easter. Accompany Jesus into the Garden of Gethsemane; spend time in this holy hour with the one who loved you so much that he laid down his life for you.

Walk in Her Sandals: Huldah's Story
by Stephanie Landsem

Huldah added a handful of parched grain to the pot over the fire and exchanged a worried glance with her dearest friend, Miriam. Tempers in the courtyard were coming to a boil faster than her barley porridge.

Miriam's younger son, James, had walked through the courtyard gate as the dawn trumpet sounded from the Temple. It was the first they'd seen of him since Jesus had arrived in Jerusalem four days earlier. Miriam jumped to embrace James, while her daughter Anah rushed for water to wash his feet. But Joses, his older brother and the head of the family, put down his bread, his face hardening into stubborn lines.

Joses was broad of shoulder and handsome. He wore the fine robes of a scribe, and his hair and beard were always perfectly trimmed and scented. James was taller than his older brother, but his hair and beard could use a comb and scissors. Huldah cringed as Joses rose to his feet and confronted James in silence. This wouldn't end well for the two brothers. And that meant Miriam would suffer.

The pot beside Huldah came to a boil. Her husband—blessed be his memory—had often called her slow-witted, and perhaps she was, but she understood Joses's worry for his mother. Miriam was wise and had a seeking heart, and yet—despite the stories Miriam had told her about Jesus—Huldah still couldn't understand what her friend saw in the Galilean.

Huldah gave the porridge a stir and recalled Miriam's words to her the night before. "My prayer," she had said, "is that all my children would know and love Jesus as I do." Huldah doubted anyone could change Joses's stubborn mind about Jesus. As for Anah . . .

She glanced at the woman who had married her son. Anah's ebony hair framed a gentle face, and she had a quiet dignity in the way she moved. Huldah had learned to love Anah—for her kindness, her sincerity, and her love for Ephraim that even her private nature couldn't hide—but Anah was hard to truly know. She surely sorrowed over her barren womb yet did not speak of it even to her own mother. It was impossible to guess what she thought of Jesus.

"I'm only asking for my mother's help with the feast," James was saying to Joses. "Jesus asked us to prepare the Passover, and we need her to serve it."

Joses recoiled as if he'd been slapped. "Don't be absurd. She's your mother, not a servant."

Huldah exchanged a surprised glance with Anah. Joses was right. For Miriam to serve strangers at table—and the

Passover, no less—was an insult. If they needed servants, they should have hired them days ago.

Joses pulled himself to his full height. "Mother will celebrate the Passover with her family, not serving a man who condemns the scribes as hypocrites."

Huldah grimaced and kept her eyes on her work. So Jesus had hurt Joses's pride as well as taken his brother and mother. Still, Joses was the head of his family and was right to want his mother with them for Passover.

"I'm happy to serve him, Joses," Miriam spoke up.

Joses turned on his mother. "The blasphemer speaks and you run to him like a . . . a slave! What hold does this man have on you both? What authority?"

James stepped up, "He is the M—"

"Don't say it." Joses snapped, holding up his hand as if to block the word. "I've heard it enough from her." He jerked his head at Miriam.

Huldah's heart wrenched. Poor Miriam. It must hurt to hear her sons argue.

Joses's voice was strained, his jaw clenched. "What about us, Mother? What about Veronica, and your grandchild, and me? Don't we mean anything to you?"

"Of course you do." Miriam's voice held tears.

"Jesus is dangerous. Think of what he did at the Temple! And now he's wanted by the Sanhedrin." Joses shook his head. "I have no choice but to forbid you"—his glance caught Veronica as well as his mother—"all of you, to help him. He'll not have our bread or wine, or even a sprig of herb."

"But, my son—" Miriam stuttered.

"I will not speak of this again." With that, Joses slammed out the courtyard gate.

Huldah went to her friend, and Miriam slumped into her arms. "If he would only listen to me." But Joses wouldn't change his mind; they all knew that. And if he'd forbidden his mother to help James, that was that.

James rubbed his hand over his beard. "What am I to do now? Peter and John are preparing the room and the sacrifice. Am I supposed to bake the bread and serve it myself?"

Huldah hid a twitch of a smile at the thought of James measuring flour and kneading dough like a woman. And wasn't it typical of men not to think ahead? But as Huldah looked into Miriam's miserable face, her heart went out to her friend. "Let me serve," she said without thinking.

James jerked his head up. "Would you?"

Miriam met her eyes, "Can you?"

Anah, silent during the exchange between her brothers, spoke up. "How will you find wheat at this late hour, and the wine? The shops were bare yesterday."

Huldah hadn't thought of that. She sent up a silent prayer. "The Lord will provide, just as he did in the desert." She put her hand on Anah's arm. "Will you—could you . . . help me, my dear?"

Anah looked unsure. Was she too against Jesus? Or just unwilling to go against Joses? "Ephraim won't forbid it." Huldah added. Her son was not nearly as difficult as Joses. "And we will see and hear Jesus."

Anah nodded, although she didn't seem pleased. Huldah felt a rush of relief. With Anah's help, and a few small miracles from the Most High, they could prepare the meal and perhaps find out what Miriam and James saw in Jesus that the rest of them did not.

As the first stars appeared in the night sky, Huldah arrived at the house James had described. The upper room, where the dinner would take place, held a low table surrounded by couches, just enough to seat Jesus and his twelve followers. Huldah pushed through a curtained doorway to a small covered porch. Anah, bent over the fire where a lamb roasted, looked up in relief.

Huldah set down her load of grain, vegetables, and wine and collapsed on a stool. "I had to go to three places for wheat." She had scoured the marketplace for the wheat, fresh herbs, and vegetables to accompany the lamb.

"How did you buy it all?" Anah asked, inspecting the wine, a better vintage than even Joses would have purchased.

Huldah wiped her damp forehead. James had given her what little money he had, but it hadn't gone far enough. "The Lord provided."

Anah raised her brows. "The Lord and all the coins you've saved."

"Nothing good comes without sacrifice." Huldah answered with a tired smile. She had spent all she had, but Miriam would want her to give Jesus the best. She pushed herself up on her aching feet. "They'll be here soon. I'll get started on the bread."

As she added salt to the wheat flour, Huldah's anticipation grew, and she forgot her aching feet. Miriam had told her so much of what Jesus had said and done. But was he really the Messiah? *Most High God, open my eyes to see and my ears to hear.*

The voices of the men drifted through the heavy curtain. "They're here." Huldah rose to her feet, her knees creaking. "I'll take in the water."

Huldah took up the wide bowl of water and a linen cloth for the men to immerse and dry their hands. With a deep breath, she parted the curtain. Although there were a dozen men there, mostly strangers, one man commanded her attention.

Jesus. That had to be him.

His appearance wasn't remarkable. Of average height, perhaps a bit thin, with a tunic of typical cut and quality for a Galilean. And yet, he was different. Perhaps it was the way he stood—the quiet and stillness of him. Or how the other men watched him, even as they found their places to recline at the table.

She put the water and towel on the table and returned to the porch for the bitter herbs, vinegar, and vegetables that would start the meal. As the men began the ritual, she and Anah worked together to finish baking the rounds of unleavened bread over the fire.

When it was time, Huldah entered the room. She poured the first cup of wine at Jesus' right side. But Jesus did not reach for the wine or recite the blessing. Instead, he rose and removed his outer garments. Huldah stepped back from the table and stared. Jesus tied the towel around his waist like a servant and took up the water bowl. Huldah stood with her hands hanging at her sides and her mouth open. What was this man doing?

Jesus went to Peter, knelt before him, and began to loosen the big fisherman's sandals. Peter exclaimed, "Master, are you going to wash my feet?"

Jesus removed one sandal. "You don't understand now, my friend, but later you will."

"You will never wash my feet." Simon Peter stated, crossing his arms over his chest.

Jesus pulled off the other sandal. "Unless I do, you will have no inheritance with me."

Huldah knew she should return to the other room, but her feet were rooted to the floor. Miriam had warned her Jesus wasn't like other men—but this!

Peter jumped up. "Then not only my feet, but my hands and head as well."

Huldah saw the curtain move behind her, and Anah's face peek out. "What is he doing?" Anah mouthed, staring at Jesus.

Huldah shook her head, bewildered.

". . . has no need except to have his feet washed," Jesus was saying. "So you are clean, but not all." Jesus' eyes rested on a disciple halfway down the table. The man fidgeted nervously, not meeting Jesus' gaze.

A shiver passed over Huldah's neck like a cold breeze. *That must be Judas*, she thought. Huldah had heard Miriam speak of Judas—but why did this disciple look so uneasy at Jesus words?

Jesus brought the water bowl to the next disciple. "If I, your master and teacher, have washed your feet, you ought to wash one another's feet. As I have done for you, you should also do."

Huldah held her breath. What did he mean? He was talking about more than washing feet, even she knew that. And something about his words resonated within her. They weren't shocking; they were right and true and powerful.

Anah whispered, breaking into Huldah's thoughts. "Help me with the bread."

Huldah went to the fire and pulled out the hot bread, but she hardly felt the heat. *As I have done for you, you should also do.* She knew about serving others; it was her place to serve her son and her family, to cook and clean. Yet Jesus' words seemed to elevate these small tasks. She felt as though everything she did, from washing to cleaning and changing little Benjamin's soiled clothing, was suddenly worth more. *She* was worth more. How did so few words mean so much to her? Is this what Miriam meant—that Jesus seemed to speak to her very heart?

She brought out the bread and set it on the table while Anah served the lamb and the puree of figs and dried apricots. Jesus had dressed and reclined again at the head of the table. A profound silence fell as he took up the bread. Instead of the usual blessing, he spoke new words. "Take this and eat it. This is my body, which will be given up for you."

The disciples looked at each other, confusion written on their faces as they took the bread and ate it in silence. Then, Jesus took the cup of wine: "Drink this, all of you, for this is my blood of the covenant, which will be shed on behalf of many for the forgiveness of sins."

Huldah backed through the curtain and into Anah, listening at the gap. "What does it all mean?" she asked.

Anah frowned. "Only the Most High can forgive our sins," she whispered. "And he requires a sacrifice."

Huldah peeked out the curtain with her. Yes, everyone knew that. That's what the lamb was for, and the bulls and goats sacrificed in the Temple each day.

Anah moved back to the porch, but Huldah remained, watching the men eat. She pondered Jesus' words. Yes, she wasn't as quick of mind as Anah or as wise as Miriam. Yet, when he spoke, her heart quickened and she could understand his words in a way she had never known before. And she wanted to hear more. She took up the wine jar and edged into the room.

Jesus spoke again as he dipped the bitter herbs. "I say to you, one of you will betray me."

Huldah jerked back. Betray him? To the Sanhedrin?

The disciples all spoke at once. "Surely not I?"

"It is not me!"

Amid the discord, the one called Judas leaned in toward Jesus. Huldah bent close to hear. "Surely it is not I, Rabbi?" his voice was flat, his eyes hooded.

"You have said so," came Jesus' reply.

Judas's face changed, as if suddenly a shadow moved within him. A chill ran over Huldah. She held the wine jar to her chest like a shield and backed away from the table. Would this man really betray Jesus to the authorities? He, who had followed Jesus, and seen him perform miracles?

The disciples began to sing the Hallel. All except Judas. He rose and, as silent as a shadow, slipped out the back door. Huldah looked to Jesus. He was watching Judas, a sadness in his eyes that made her own heart ache. Where was Judas going in the middle of the Passover meal? And why was Jesus not calling him back?

Worry for Jesus warred with wonder at what she had heard from him tonight. Miriam had told her to listen with her ears and hear with her heart. She had, and now she knew this man, Jesus, was sent by God as surely as she knew something terrible was about to happen to him. And Jesus knew it too.

Take this, and eat. This is my body, which will be given up for you. . . . This is my blood of the covenant, which will be shed on behalf of many for the forgiveness of sins.

The lamb had been sacrificed for the Passover. But Jesus had told them his body and blood would be the sacrifice. What did it all mean? And what part would Judas have in what would happen next?

A cold certainty grew inside Huldah. Nothing good comes without sacrifice, she had said to Anah, and it was true. Something told her that very soon there would be another sacrifice—not just a lamb but something infinitely greater and more precious.

Unwrap the Gift of Generosity
by Pat Gohn

As he spoke the words of institution at that last Passover feast with his disciples, Jesus anticipated the fulfillment of God's redemptive plan and the ultimate sacrifice he would make in just a few short hours, a gesture that would change the course of human history. This act of love, this supreme generosity, reveals something about God himself: God loves, and so he gives (see Jn 3:16–17). God is a generous giver; Jesus is the greatest gift the world has ever known! How can we respond adequately to such an amazing gift? —Kelly Wahlquist

The gift of a woman's generosity is linked to her receptive nature. As we receive God's love, we too are called to give generously. Generosity and the gift of self, or self-donation, are linked. Within the documents of Vatican II, the Church teaches that we who are designed by so generous and loving a God cannot fully find ourselves except through making a sincere gift of ourselves (see *Gaudium et Spes*, 24).

To better cultivate the gift of generosity, and to learn to make a gift of ourselves to others, we take lessons from Jesus. At the Last Supper on Holy Thursday, Jesus teaches about the gift of self as he washes the feet of his friends. Jesus shocks them with this humble gesture. Yet what he did next was even more incredible.

At the meal, Jesus instituted the Holy Eucharist, offering his very Body and Blood to his friends under the signs of bread and wine. His words, "This is my body which is given for you," would ring in the minds and hearts of his apostles whenever they reflected on the fullness of his sacrifice completed on the Cross. He made a gift of himself in a most extraordinary way.

Self-sacrificing, self-donating love is the root of all vocations. All of us, in some way, must come to exemplify Jesus' words: *This is my body which is given for you*. Each of us within our respective vocations are also called to offer up our bodies for the good of others and to glorify God.

To be given in marriage, or to be given in religious life, is to lay down one's life for the spouse, for the beloved. For single women, who may not be given to religious life or marriage, the call to generous love remains ever present. After all, Jesus was a single person too! He proves the path to generous self-donation is laying down one's life for his friends.

"We love, because he first loved us" (1 Jn 4:19).

Regardless of our vocation, let us first *believe and receive the generous gift of God*, which is Jesus himself. Then let us *share the generous gift of God* lavishly. We were made for this!

As you come to Holy Thursday, consider your gift of generosity:

- How might you live these words of Jesus more generously? "Love one another as I have loved you" (Jn 15:12; see also Jn 13:34).

- When was the last time you took on a lowly chore and did it joyfully out of love for Jesus? "When he had washed their feet . . . and resumed his place, [Jesus] said to them, 'Do you know what I have done to you?'" (Jn 13:12).

- How often in our lives do we as women live out this phrase with a unique brand of generosity? "This is my body which is given for you" (Lk 22:19).

Reflect on the Meaning: Holy Thursday
by Teresa Tomeo

No doubt we have all heard at various times in our lives that it is better to give than to receive. St. Paul repeats this idea in the book of Acts: "In all things I have shown you that by so toiling one must help the weak, remembering the words of the Lord Jesus, how he said, 'It is more blessed to give than to receive'" (Acts 20:35).

"It is in giving that we receive," one popular Franciscan prayer reminds us. More recently, St. John Paul II took it one step further: "We don't find ourselves until we lose ourselves in Christ." The way to sainthood, then, is to cultivate a generous heart. Being generous is good for us.

I learned this lesson the hard way in what I call my "holy cannoli moment." In my Italian family, like those from many other ethnic backgrounds, food is a big part of expressing generosity and hospitality. It was the summer of 1981, and I was the Helen Reddy "I Am Woman, Hear Me Roar" type, a recent college graduate who had no intention of getting married—or, if I ever did, no way was I going to marry an Italian American man. I had dated a few in high school and college, hoping they would be like my dad. Invariably I was disappointed.

You see, my father was way ahead of his time. Yes, he loved his Italian heritage, but he didn't like the way some Italian men treated women. He had seen his own mother disrespected frequently and knew instinctively that she deserved better. When we moved to Michigan from New Jersey, he encouraged his wife, who missed her own large Italian American family terribly, to get involved outside the home, and he encouraged his three daughters to get an education so we could both make a difference in the world and take care of ourselves whether or not we decided to marry.

When my brother-in-law introduced me to a coworker of his, Dominick (who just happened to be a handsome engineer, like my father), I took a chance and went out with him, and soon realized I'd finally found "the one." He was supportive of my career goals and, well, was just a pretty great guy. I quickly fell head over heels in love with him.

The feeling was mutual, and within a few short months we decided to head to Dom's hometown in Pennsylvania so he could introduce me to his parents. Well, what started out as a get-together soon turned into a backyard barbecue block party with dozens and dozens of relatives and friends. It was like an Italian version of the engagement party scene in *My Big Fat Greek Wedding*, minus the Bundt cake.

When we arrived, my future in-laws greeted me warmly, and we all sat down around their large kitchen table. I noticed as we walked in that the counters were filled with all sorts of delectable homemade Italian pastries, a familiar scene in any Italian American home when a family get-together is right around the corner. "Are you hungry?" asked Dominick's mother. "How about a little something to eat?"

Now, all my life I have been asked this question, dozens of times, by aunts and grandmothers and the other women in my family. I know very well that these are really rhetorical questions—that the only reasonable response is to pick up a fork and dig in!

But what did I say to my future mother-in-law? "No, thanks. I'm not really hungry."

The room fell silent. My future mother-in-law had a look of shock on her face, as though I had lost my mind. I felt Dominick nudge my leg under the table. Since when does the issue of hunger have anything to do with eating? I should have known better.

To this day, I don't know what I was thinking. Maybe it was the nervousness of meeting the future in-laws. My father-in-law gently rescued me. "Oh, come on now," he coaxed, smiling. "It's been a long haul from Michigan. Surely you could use a few Pignoli cookies or a cannoli or maybe a piece of Cassata cake that Mary just whipped up for you?"

Quickly I recovered my composure. "Oh, sure. A cannoli or a piece of Cassata cake sounds great," I mumbled. As I ate the delicious treats that were placed in front of me, I did my best to make up the lost ground by raving to Mary about her cannoli. "Did you use ricotta cheese or whipped cream in the filling, or both? How did you get your cannoli shells to come out so light and crisp and not greasy?"

Instantly I realized that my job in that moment was to let Dominick's mom bless me with her particular love language. As she shared with me her culinary secrets, a kinship began to form between us that grew richer through the years. And it all began with the gift of her attentive presence. It was my "cannoli moment."

Now think about the women of Bethany, Martha and Mary. Yes, Martha was "giving" her all, or so she thought, by preparing a wonderful meal for her awesome guest, the Lord himself. But in that moment Jesus was offering her something far more valuable: an opportunity to join her sister, Mary, to sit at the feet of the King, and to receive his generous heart full of love and his words of wisdom and truth.

"But the Lord answered her, 'Martha, Martha, you are anxious and troubled about many things; one thing is needful. Mary has chosen the good portion, which shall not be taken away from her'" (Lk 10:41–42).

That experience with my now mother in-law of more than thirty-two years has taught me a great deal about having the spirit of true generosity. May we all learn to be more like the

Marys in our lives and to remember how it is as important to receive graciously as it is to give.

Just as Teresa learned an important lesson about receptive generosity in her "cannoli moment," Peter had a similar teachable moment when he encountered his Lord standing before him, intent on washing Peter's feet—the task of the lowest servant of any household. As you ponder today's gospel, think about how you would have responded, had you been out of Peter's shoes!—Kelly Wahlquist

Lectio for Holy Thursday

Read John 13:1–20, and read it a second time more slowly. Then read it for a third time, noting the words or thoughts that jump out at you.

> Now before the festival of the Passover, when Jesus knew that his hour had come to depart from this world to the Father, having loved his own who were in the world, he loved them to the end. And during supper, when the devil had already put it into the heart of Judas Iscariot, Simon's son, to betray him, Jesus, knowing that the Father had given all things into his hands, and that he had come from God and was going to God, rose from supper, laid aside his garments, and girded himself with a towel. Then he poured water into a basin and began to wash the disciples' feet, and to wipe them with the towel with which he was girded. He came to Simon Peter; and Peter said to him, "Lord, do you wash my feet?" Jesus answered him, "What I am doing you do not know but afterward you will understand." Peter said to him, "You shall never wash my feet." Jesus answered him, "If I do not wash you, you have no part in me." Simon Peter said to him, "Lord, not my feet only but also my hands and my head!" Jesus said to him, "He who has bathed does not need to wash, except for his feet, but he is clean all over; and you are clean, but not all of you." For he knew who was to betray him; that was why he said, "You are not all clean."

> When he had washed their feet, and taken his garments, and resumed his place, he said to them, "Do you know what I have done to you? You call me Teacher and Lord; and you are right, for so I am. If I then, your Lord and Teacher, have washed your feet, you also ought to wash one another's feet. For I have given you an example, that you also should do as I have done to you. Truly, truly, I say to you, a servant is not greater than his master, nor is he who sent greater than he who sent him. If you know these things, blessed are you if you do them. I am not speaking of you all; I know whom I have chosen; it is that the scripture may be fulfilled, 'He who ate my bread has lifted his heel against me.' I tell you this now, before it takes place, that when it does take place you may believe that I am he. Truly, truly, I say to you, he who receives any one whom I send receives me; and he who receives me receives him who sent me."

Now, ask yourself:

- What do I hear? (Write down the words or phrases that stand out to you as you read.)

- What does it mean? (Write down what you think about those words, or why you think they're important.)

- What is Jesus saying to me? (Write what you hear Jesus saying into your heart, and respond to him.)

Questions for Group Discussion
by Dr. Carol Younger

1. *Enter the Scripture.* Jeremiah's words stir hearts: "I will write [the new covenant] upon their hearts" (Jer 31:33). Jesus says that the chalice *is* the new covenant; the time is now. The apostles know this is a moment charged with love: Jesus is giving his life to them in this meal. Receiving the Eucharist can be a renewal of faith in Jesus, or a new awareness of belonging to Catholic life. Recall a time

when receiving Holy Communion at Mass startled you with its power to move you to tears. Can you share part of that experience with your group?

2. *Walk in Her Sandals*. "Nothing good comes without sacrifice," Huldah says, just before preparing the bread for the Last Supper, the Passover. Her generous sacrifice to buy the meal's supplies is a gift to her grieving friend Miriam and the others—and the graces of that gift were multiplied in the hands of Jesus. Sometimes when we generously give and someone benefits, God allows us to see the grace that comes from our generosity. Share with the group a time when you gave, God blessed that gift, and the receiver was twice blessed with your gift.

3. *Unwrap the Gift*. The very young child sees a beautifully wrapped gift and gets excited. An older child tears off the wrappings, eager to get the gift inside the wrapped box. The adult sees and loves the giver of the gift, rather than the gift. God's generous graces in wrappings bring us to himself: the Gift and the Giver. As spiritual children, we see the gift wrap in the Church, the beautiful liturgies. Growing in understanding God's generosity, we begin to desire the gift inside the wrapping: escape from sin, heaven, and sacramental grace. Later, when we know Jesus better through prayer, we want him instead of the gift wrap. Can you speak about the "wrapping" that first invited you into a personal relationship with Jesus? What gifts did he give you that satisfied your spiritual longings? When was it that you knew you had fallen in love with Jesus himself, the ultimate Gift and the Giver?

4. *Reflect on the Meaning*. Generosity is connected to giving and receiving, though receiving isn't often associated with being generous. We bring meals to friends who are ill, who are shut in, or who are new mothers. To give and receive food demonstrates two central truths of being human: (1) we are dependent on food for life and (2)

sharing food connects us to each other in a spiritual and familial way. Jesus presents himself as Food in the Last Supper. We are dependent on him for both temporal and eternal life. We are connected to him and to each other in his food, his Body, Blood, Soul, and Divinity. When you receive him in Holy Communion, how are you generous? For what temporal gifts do you thank him? For what spiritual, needs, especially for family or friends, do you ask him?

Walking in the New Evangelization
by Kelly Wahlquist

As we conclude this chapter, think about what new insights or "God prompts" you have experienced as you reflected on the experiences of these women. Here are a couple of ways you can continue to reflect upon what you have discovered in the coming week!

Contemplate Your Own Gifts

Jesus says, "I will not leave you desolate: I will come to you" (Jn 14:18). Though the apostles hear him, they cannot fully grasp what he is saying. The fear and grief that comes with not wanting to lose the one they loved most has them struggling to understand.

Oftentimes we worry about future events because we fear loss, pain, or the unknown. It is in times such as this that we must remember what Jesus said: he is with us now, and he will be there in the future, in our pain, problems, and struggles. What events in your future are you worrying about? What do you need from Jesus to face them *with him*? Ask him for that gift, and then say, "Jesus, I trust in you," and let it go.

Faith in Action

Generosity asks us to give of self, not just of the excess we have of time or talent, but also of the part of us that takes sacrifice. Volunteer to prepare at least two meals for someone who is housebound or ill, or volunteer to be a Eucharistic minister to the housebound or ill. Offer the time, the preparation, and the driving involved as part of your gift, your charity to God. Be generous with God.

3.

The Gift of Sensitivity

(Good Friday)

A Moment to Ponder

by Kelly Wahlquist

On Good Friday, we read from John's account of the last day in the life of Christ (see Jn 18:1–19:42). The "beloved disciple" recounts each excruciating detail of the ordeal as only he can, as the only apostle who stayed with the women. In his account we meet the inquisitive maid who recognized Peter at the door of the high priest's house as well as the three Marys standing by the cross. Curiously absent are two other women: the wife of Pilate, who had warned her husband not to harm Jesus, and Veronica, the woman we will read about in today's story, whose story is found only in sacred tradition.

Each of these women embodied great sensitivity and intuition, which led them to act courageously to bear witness to Jesus' fate and to do what they could to alleviate the Lord's suffering. As you relive these events in scripture and ponder their deeper meaning in your own life, I pray that it will reawaken within you a resolve to use your own gifts to meet Jesus in his "distressing disguise" in the crosses and burdens in your own life, to comfort and encourage those around you, and to lead them closer to him.

Enter the Scripture
by Sarah Christmyer

As we leave the intimate space of the Garden of Gethsemane, we follow our Lord on the final day of his life, as it was captured by those closest to him (Mt 27; Mk 15; Lk 22:66–23:49; Jn 18:1–19:42).

The day we call Good Friday both begins and ends in darkness, in a garden.

The first garden is a quiet place among olive trees, a place Jesus has often gone with his disciples to pray. He leads them there after the Last Supper, carrying with him the weight of the fallen world and the knowledge of what it will cost to put things right. He is motivated by love.

The garden is called Gethsemane: "olive press." There, crushed olives were pressed beneath heavy stone slabs until the oil flowed out to be gathered in clay jars. It's a fitting place for Jesus' nighttime agony. Luke describes his sweat "like great drops of blood falling down upon the ground" (Lk 22:44)—as though the Lord himself is in an olive press. Olive oil was treasured for providing light, healing, and nourishment. Jesus, crushed, will be all of these things for the world.

The second garden is Golgotha, "place of the skull." In a gruesome parody of the garden on the Mount of Olives, crosses are planted instead of trees. The sun goes black while the Son hangs on the cross. There, "the true light that enlightens every man" (Jn 1:9), that "shines in the darkness" (Jn 1:5), is lifted up for all to see. "Behold the man!" Good Friday is a day of contradiction, a horrifying day we still call "good."

In the long hours between one garden and the other, Jesus is arrested, falsely accused, and sentenced to death. He walks, carrying his own cross, to Golgotha.

This is the Via Dolorosa—"The Way of Suffering." For centuries, pilgrims have traced Jesus' steps from the Fortress Antonia, where he was sentenced by Pilate, for a little under half a mile through the streets of Old Jerusalem to the place of his crucifixion and burial. It was outside the city walls in Jesus' day, but as the city grew, other walls were built, and today it sits at the heart of Jerusalem, enveloped by the Church of the Holy Sepulchre. Walking this road today, one is struck by how public much of the Passion was. Jesus was scourged in an open square where all could see his back flayed, the pain, and the blood running freely. The streets through which he carried the cross are narrow. There he would be in easy reach of onlookers who might touch, jostle, or spit—or offer a towel to wipe his face.

To the extent that we execute prisoners today, it's done in private. But in Jesus' day, crucifixion was deliberately public, deliberately horrifying. Death came slowly, sometimes over several days, through the loss of blood and asphyxiation. Sometimes bones were broken to hasten the process.

Cicero called crucifixion the "cruelest and most disgusting penalty."[1] Josephus called it "the most pitiable of deaths."[2] The reason crosses were planted outside the city walls was not to keep them out of sight, as you might think, but so that every traveler in and out of the city would be confronted with their strong message: rebel, this horror awaits you too.

In the Church of the Holy Sepulchre, a large mosaic shows Christ lying on the cross before it is raised upright. Standing above him, shrouded in black and filling most of the scene, is Mary. Her face reflects her soul, which has been pierced by pain and sorrow that are hard to imagine. The grief must be crippling—yet she stands. Also near the cross, we learn from the gospels, are several other women and John. All the disciples except this one whom "[Jesus] loved" (Jn 19:26) have fled in fear. But "perfect love casts out fear" (1 Jn 4:18). It lends courage to compassion.

It is John who tells us Jesus' final act, the thing that enables him to say that "it is finished" (Jn 19:30). Seeing Mary and John standing there, Jesus gives them to each other: "'Woman, behold, your son!' Then he [says] to the disciple, 'Behold, your mother!'" (Jn 19:26–27). With these words, the Lord entrusts all of his disciples, present and future, to the spiritual motherhood of Mary (see *CCC*, 501, 964).

"It is finished," the Lord says—not "it's finally over" but "it is finished." Completed! "For this I was born, and for this I have come into the world, to bear witness to the truth," he said earlier to Pilate.

"What is truth?" Pilate answered (Jn 18:37–38).

Perhaps we are about to find out that God loves us to the end, whatever that end might be. That no sin or death, however hideous, has power to defeat him or his plan. The thing that is "finished" is finished by God, not by man. Jesus died so we can live.

Did Mary know this, then? Like Abraham, did she believe her promised Son could be raised again (see Heb 11:19)? On Good Friday, we have no answers. We call it "good" only in retrospect. Today we enter the darkness with Mary, with the beloved disciple, with the women huddled in silent vigil before the Lord.

Our Good Friday liturgy includes the Veneration of the Cross. The Reproaches that are sung plunge us into the story:

> O, my people, what have I done to you?
> How have I offended you? Answer me! . . .
> I raised you to the height of majesty,
> but you have raised me high on a cross.

What can we say to that? Our hearts break—and the liturgy guides our response:

> Holy is God!
> Holy and mighty!
> Holy immortal One, have mercy on us!

Jesus knew where he was headed when he entered Jerusalem on a donkey, hailed as a king. He knew the way to glory lay through humiliation and pain. And yet he carried that cross.

> We worship you, Lord,
> We venerate your cross,
> We praise your resurrection.
>   Through the cross
>   You brought joy to the world.

On Good Friday, look at Jesus and adore the Cross; he did this for you.

Walk in Her Sandals: Veronica's Story
by Stephanie Landsem

As we behold our dying Lord upon the cross, that awful instrument of torture, our sensibilities cause us to steel ourselves against the horror. Part of us pulls back, unwilling to face the reality of it, to face the anguish and the gore. But on that day, there were two women who did not look away, did not hold back. The first was Jesus' Mother, and the other, according to sacred tradition, was a woman named Veronica. —Kelly Wahlquist

Veronica pressed through the crowd, just avoiding a stout matron pushing past her. The narrow side street near the Gennath Gate teemed with well-dressed Pharisees, ragged shepherds, and gawking pilgrims from throughout Judea. She covered her nose with her head covering as the pungent scents of sheep dung and warm bodies rose up around her.

I shouldn't be here. She should be home, helping Anah, not in the upper city alone. She'd need to explain her absence to Joses when she returned home.

"Stay close to home today," Joses had said that morning as he ate bread and almonds. "They've arrested the Galilean." He frowned into his cup of goat's milk. "Now he's put all his followers in danger."

Veronica had not answered but pulled her needle through the hem of her new linen head covering as her heart went out to her husband. Joses was still hurt that his mother and brother had left him to follow a stranger, and a Galilean at that. Still, didn't Joses wonder who Jesus really was?

Veronica glanced across the courtyard, where Zilpah, her husband's grandmother, sat in the sunshine, her eyes closed, her lips moving in prayer. Miriam had left at first light to find Mary and the disciples. Was Zilpah praying for Jesus? Or for her daughter and James, who might be in danger this morning because of a Galilean's reckless talk?

A high-pitched wail made Veronica drop her sewing and rush to the courtyard. Benjamin lay face down on the dirty ground. He pushed himself up, his chubby hands rubbing over his face, leaving streaks of dirt and grime. A scrape oozed red on his cheek.

"Is he hurt?" Joses asked, kneeling beside them.

Veronica gathered the whimpering toddler in her arms and pulled him close. His cries stopped. She wiped his face with the corner of her robe. "Just a scratch." She kissed the tip of her son's nose and set him on his unsteady feet. He smiled a watery smile, and it warmed her heart that she could comfort him with her touch.

If only she could soothe Joses's hurt as easily.

Joses ruffled Benjamin's hair before gathering his rolls of parchment for his work at the Temple. Veronica followed him to the gate. "Joses?" Perhaps she could soften his heart toward his brother. "Don't you wonder if, perhaps, your mother and brother are right? All he's done, healing the sick, and the man who was dead in Bethany?"

Joses scowled. "My mother and brother have been taken in by a fraud, Veronica." He shouldered through the gate. "They will find that out soon enough."

After Joses left, she washed the cups and put wood on the fire, restless and distracted. Who was right about Jesus—the ones who called him a liar and blasphemer or the ones who called him the Messiah? And what was happening to Jesus and his followers now?

She knew one place that she could find answers.

When Benjamin climbed onto Zilpah's lap and stuck his thumb in his mouth, Veronica pulled her new head covering over her hair and shoulders. She tucked the leftover bread from their morning meal into her tunic and kissed the top of Benjamin's head. "Be good for Grandmother. I'll be back soon."

At the Temple gate, the beggars claimed their usual places. Veronica smiled at the old man with twisted legs and a toothless grin, giving him the softest round of bread. She distributed the rest among the other unfortunates: the gaunt woman with a baby at her breast and the blind man with grasping hands. An unfamiliar girl, not much older than Veronica, took the last round with one hand, ripping it with her teeth. Her other arm hung shriveled and useless at her side.

As with all of Jerusalem, the beggars spoke of Jesus. The thin-faced mother bowed her head. "He spoke for the poor and cured the sick. Now they say everything he did was tricks and lies."

"Tricks?" The girl with the withered hand huffed. "They weren't tricks. He is from the Lord."

"How do you know?" The question flew from Veronica's mouth. How could this girl know so surely when so many others—learned men and holy women—didn't know what to think?

The girl turned to Veronica. "I was in Bethany. I saw a man come out of his tomb after being dead four days." She took a deep breath, her eyes shining. "Who has power over death but the Lord himself?"

Veronica stared at the girl. She'd heard the story at the well and from Miriam, and every time a shiver went over her skin. When Veronica's mother had died just before she married Joses, she had sat beside her cold body and wept. If

Jesus could bring life to the dead, surely he could not be from the evil one?

The girl's voice turned bitter as she waved her good hand at the Temple. "The Sanhedrin wouldn't know the Messiah if he was right under their noses."

As the girl returned to her place along the wall, Veronica couldn't help but admire her faith. Perhaps if she could see Jesus herself, she would believe as strongly.

The toothless man swallowed his bread. "He may be from the Lord, but I saw them take him to Pilate." His voice was bleak and hopeless. "He's already carrying his cross out of the city."

Veronica's heart turned in her chest. How could they crucify him, when he performed such miracles? How could they kill a man who could raise the dead? If only she'd been able to see him, just a glimpse. But it was too late.

Unless . . . if Veronica was quick, she could get to the Gennath Gate before he left the city. Perhaps she could find out for herself if he was a fraud, a prophet, or something else entirely, something no one understood.

Now, as the crowd jostled and pushed in the winding streets near the Gennath Gate, she understood Joses's warning. She raised herself up on her toes but still couldn't see over the shoulders of the men in front of her.

"He's coming!" A boy shouted.

Veronica's heart pounded in her throat as she ducked under the arm of a well-dressed Greek and pushed closer.

There, in the street, a man carried a cross.

Her breath caught in her throat. Blood and dirt streaked his tunic. His back was bent, his steps torturously slow. Upon his head a wreath of thorns—thorns the size of a man's finger—pierced his temple and forehead. Blood dripped down his face, into his eyes, and over his swollen lips. This was the man she'd come to see, Jesus of Nazareth.

Next to Veronica, an old woman began to keen. Beside her, a mother and what looked like her two daughters wept.

Veronica stood as still as stone, her eyes on the man before her as he stopped and turned his beaten face to the weeping women.

Would he speak to them, these women who mourned?

"Daughters of Jerusalem, do not weep for me." His voice rasped as though his throat were as dry as sand. "Weep instead for yourselves and for your children. The days are coming when people will say, 'Blessed are the barren, the wombs that never bore and the breasts that never nursed.'"

His words sent a shiver over Veronica's skin. She tried to move closer, but a boy shoved her and the crowd pushed her along like a rock in a stream. She scrambled back toward the women, but Jesus had already turned from them.

As she wondered at his words, Jesus staggered and fell to his knees, the weight of the cross biting into his shoulders and back. Shouts and jeers erupted around her, but her eyes were drawn to a woman, lurching out of the crowd with a cry of anguish. She was older, about the age of Veronica's own mother when she died. Veronica knew her, not from Miriam's description, but from the pain etched on the woman's face—a pain so profound, it could only belong to Jesus' mother, Mary of Nazareth.

Mary fell to her knees in front of Jesus, her hands reaching out to him, but before she could touch him, a trio of soldiers descended on her, wrenched her to her feet and hurled her back into the crowd. Her red-rimmed eyes met Veronica's across the gulf of the dusty street.

Veronica's heart wrenched in her chest. She looked at Jesus again and suddenly saw him anew. He wasn't a man covered in blood; he wasn't a criminal. He was a son, loved by Mary in every way that Veronica loved Benjamin. Veronica blinked back tears. How could Mary bear it?

Jesus pushed himself to his feet with a groan of agony. Sweat veiled his face and ran into his red-rimmed eyes. Her heart called out for her to comfort this man, Jesus, as a mother would. But what could she do? She had nothing to offer him.

She thought of Joses and how angry he would be if he knew she was here. But she had to do something—anything.

Her mouth was as dry as a potsherd, but with a jerk, she pulled off the veil that covered her hair and stepped into the street. The jeers of the boys and the shouts of the soldiers faded. She heard only her heartbeat, saw only the face of the man in front of her. She pressed the white linen gently to his bruised and broken face, wishing she could wipe away the pain as she removed the sweat, blood, and dirt.

As she took away the cloth, she looked into his eyes. In them, she saw not death and despair but something else she couldn't name—something akin to peace but deeper and unfathomable. A rush of warmth flowed over her and filled her. In the next instant, the soldier returned, prodding Jesus with his stick. Jesus pushed himself up and continued his torturous journey.

Veronica stepped back, into the safety of the crowd. Hardly a moment had passed, and yet it had felt like a lifetime. She leaned against the cool stone of the city wall with her soiled veil clutched to her chest. What had happened just then? What had she witnessed in a man about to die?

She caught sight of Mary, and this time she could see Miriam, Huldah, and others, supporting her as they followed Jesus out the gate. She was pulled in two directions—toward home, to kiss Benjamin's sweet face and forget she'd ever seen Jesus, but also toward the women and Jesus' suffering mother. Should she turn away from Jesus, or follow him?

The wind took the cloth in her hands, unfurling it in the breeze. She gasped and caught at the fabric, examining it more closely. The dirt and blood looked . . . it was the likeness of a man. The likeness of Jesus, just as he had appeared to her moments before—the wounds on his forehead, the tracks of his tears on his cheeks, and the mouth set in pain. Her heart pounded. Instead of the ugliness of death written in blood and tears, there was beauty in his face, beauty and love and a meaning that she didn't understand.

She should be afraid. The likeness of a man went against the most holy commandment. Any Jew would be outraged to see it. And yet she felt as if all her questions had been answered. She had been looking for Jesus, but as she gazed at the cloth, she realized that Jesus had been looking for her, just for her. She didn't understand who he was or why he sought her, but she knew she must follow him; and to follow him, she must follow his mother.

She hurried through the gate. The sun burned hot as she left the shade of the city, and a dry wind blew from the east. Her breath came fast, and sweat trickled down her back as she climbed the narrow path that wound up a rocky hill. Above the wail of the wind, she could hear shouted orders in Latin, the ring of hammers on iron, and anguished cries.

As she crested the top, her labored breath caught in her throat. Three crosses stood against the darkening sky. Jesus was nailed to the center cross. His mother stood at his feet, bent in her private agony.

Pain pierced Veronica's heart like a thorn. Her pain, she knew, was only a shadow of what the mother of Jesus endured. Veronica stepped forward and took her place beside Mary: Mary, whose son bled on a cross and whose heart was broken as only a mother's heart can break.

Veronica clutched the veil close, and it burned like a brand on her breast.

I am just where I should be.

Unwrap the Gift of Sensitivity
by Pat Gohn

"I am just where I should be." How often have you sensed this in your own life, that God or your guardian angel had guided you through your womanly intuition to do or say something for which there was no logical explanation? And how often do you later discover it was exactly what was needed at that particular time? This

is the gift of sensitivity, which is this week's feminine gift! —Kelly Wahlquist

As women we feel things deeply, in good times and bad. The first time I watched *The Passion of the Christ*, I remember straining to see the screen through my own tears. We cry at weddings and funerals. We cry tears of solidarity with friends who are suffering. The tears are not always visible to everyone around us. Even so, we cry.

On the other hand, we women are much more than the sum of our tears. Inside us is a wellspring of strength and healing that comes with the gift of sensitivity. The glory of God comes alive in a woman's sensitivity. God's genius shows up in a woman, in a certain sense, in that a woman can see another person similar to how God sees them. "Perhaps more than men, women *acknowledge the person*, because they see persons with their hearts."[3]

Seeing with the heart is more than using the sense of sight. It is that inward glance, that intuitiveness to see beyond the exterior and to read the cues, dispositions, and circumstances that may be revealed, without the other explaining it.

True sensitivity recognizes the dignity of the other person, even if it is often hidden under pain, shame, weakness, sorrow, or sin. This makes sensitivity, as a gift inherent in women, deeper and superior to sensitivity's misunderstood and misguided relatives: overemotionalism or sappy sentimentalism.

Yet a woman's sensitivity is not just about seeing or noticing what's going on in another. Sensitivity's true power is that it moves a woman to *help*.

This gift of sensitivity is why so many women choose to marry and become mothers, or to become trained in the helping professions. They see the suffering of others, the need for nurture and healing, and take action to address it. Sensitivity is strength, a catalyst for healing.

Imagine the many scenes of Good Friday. Jesus is arrested and brought to Pilate, whose wife tries to intervene in the proceedings—whether for Jesus' sake, or for Pilate's, we do not know. She is ignored.

Later, Pilate has Jesus scourged and condemned. Jesus is bleeding and limping as he carries his cross along the Via Dolorosa toward his execution. We have only to reflect on the Stations of the Cross to see sensitivity on display: the women of Jerusalem who cry for Jesus along the route and reach out on behalf of his suffering. Veronica breaks through the crowds and offers a consoling moment of relief and comfort to the bloody face of Jesus, respite from his excruciating labor. Most importantly, Jesus has the heart-to-heart meeting with his Mother, Mary.

Lastly, witness the women at the cross, with John. They cannot save Jesus, but they stay with him. He will not die alone. Their fidelity is some consolation; they are doing the hard thing despite their tears and fears. They pray for the dying and will bury the dead.

Works of mercy such as these are the fruit of sensitivity. Women do the difficult things on behalf of others—because they see with their hearts. They feel. They connect. They go and help.

Sensitivity longs to help and to heal. The glory of God in this gift sees past the ruin and the brokenness of the person to the image of the Creator reflected therein.

These women see and believe in the hidden glory of God on the bloodied visage of Jesus. Their sensitivity fuels works of mercy. Such sensitivity breeds saints.

As you come to Good Friday, consider your gift of sensitivity:

1. What was your response when you read the quotation by St. John Paul II, "Women *acknowledge the person*, because they see persons with their hearts"? Who or what did it make you think of?

2.   What good is it to stay near others when they are suffering, if it is not possible for you to relieve their pain? Have you ever experienced this "gift of presence"?

3.   Is it ever possible to be too "sensitive"? Are there any dangers in misusing the gift of sensitivity?

Reflect on the Meaning: Good Friday
by Laura Sobiech

Sensitivity is not the same as sentimentality, any more than courage is the same as fearlessness. The gift of sensitivity enables us to stand with, and stand by, without turning or flinching. This was true of the women who followed Jesus to his death, and it is true of those who are called to journey with those who are facing their own mortality. —Kelly Wahlquist

My son, Zach, was just fourteen when he was diagnosed with a rare bone cancer called osteosarcoma. The evening we found out, my mind was a jumble of thoughts as I came to grips with our new reality. Would Zach be able to play sports? Would he have a normal life? Would he be able to keep up with his schoolwork? Would he be able to go to school? And then one thought hit me with the force of a violent blow.

Zach could die from this. Every motherly instinct in me reared in agony as I imagined my son suffering and dying. It was too much. It was too terrifying.

Abruptly, in the midst of the chaos in my mind, I became aware of God's presence in the room, and a profound peace enveloped me. I knew he was asking me to trust him.

While I'd never wavered in my *belief* in God (even when I strayed from him), I struggled with *trusting* him. I was afraid he would give me something bigger than I could handle. Now though, it wasn't a matter of whether I would be given a big cross; it was simply a matter of how I would bear it. I realized that this was the moment I had spent my entire faith life training for. All of the little acts of obedient faith, the little crosses, had been to prepare me for this big cross.

"Okay," was my simple answer. "I'll trust you." And so we started down our Via Dolorosa, our way of the cross with cancer.

I watched, helpless, as the nurse pushed a needle into Zach's chest, like a tack into a bulletin board, for his first chemotherapy treatment. He turned away from me and clenched his eyes shut, in tremendous pain. I wanted to comfort him by picking him up and cuddling him, like I did when he was a little boy. But he was too old for that now. I could only stay close and pray.

Day after day, I would go to the hospital after work and spend hours sitting with Zach, trying to fill the time with cheerful conversation. After weeks of this routine, he seemed annoyed when I would walk in his hospital room door. I wondered if this teenager really wanted to spend so much time with his mom.

"Would you prefer I not come every day, Zach?" I asked. "It won't hurt my feelings if you want some space."

He thought about it for a moment. "No," he answered, "I want you here." So, I just sat with him quietly, knowing I was right where I was supposed to be.

Zach was patient in his suffering and showed remarkable courage and empathy for others throughout his battle. But after two years of fighting and the cancer continuing to progress, I wondered if he fully understood how dire his situation was. One afternoon, as we sat in the clinic exam room after another recurrence in Zach's lungs, I read through the statistics report for the latest chemotherapy the doctors were recommending. The numbers were not good; it was clear we had run out of treatments that would significantly extend his life.

Zach was cheerfully flipping through a worn-out copy of *Car and Driver* magazine. I dreaded what I had to do. "The numbers aren't good," I said, as I set the packet of information down.

"Yeah. Well, I'll just deal with stuff as it comes," he replied nonchalantly, still focused on the magazine.

"Zach, this stuff won't get rid of the cancer." I looked him in the eye to hold his attention. He set the magazine down. "Honey, you're not invincible." My heart ached as I watched the understanding play out on his face.

Eventually the cancer spread to Zach's lungs and pelvis, and we were told he had only a year to live. A few weeks later, I had it out with God. I didn't want Zach to suffer and die. But that point on the horizon we had been traveling toward— Zach living a long, cancer-free life—was unreachable; the road was gone. I didn't know what to hope for anymore, and I didn't know how to pray. I needed a new road.

"How do I do this?" I cried out to the Blessed Mother, hot tears streaming down my face.

Then a simple image filled my mind. It was of God's hand reaching down and pulling that point from the horizon up into the heavens. It was time to shift my focus to what I had always known—this life is a pilgrimage to the eternal, and our true hope should never be in anything physical; it should always be in eternity with God. And whatever road we find ourselves on can lead to eternity with Christ if we join our suffering with his.

Of course, my ultimate hope for Zach, and all of my children, had always been union with God in heaven. But as Zach's mother, how could I not beg God for my son's life? Yet, I was choosing to trust God. The two seemed to be in conflict.

"How do I pray?" I begged the Blessed Mother for guidance. Then I remembered her Son's prayer in his agony just before he was taken to be crucified. He prayed, "Father, if you are willing, remove this cup from me; nevertheless not my will, but thine be done." It was the perfect prayer of petition and submission to God's will, and I made it my own.

"I don't want Zach to die," I prayed. "But if you have another plan, then please allow his death to be for something big—one life changed forever."

Zach died almost a year later. God used Zach's life as a channel of tremendous grace into the world and, through his suffering, brought hope to millions of people across the globe.

"If any man would come after me, let him deny himself and take up his cross and follow me" (Mt 16:24). As you refelct on Laura's story about her son Zach, ask yourself: Have I ever willingly offered back to God that which was most precious to me? —Kelly Wahlquist

Lectio for Good Friday

As you contemplate this defining moment in salvation history, consider what it would have been like to be standing there with Mary, beneath the cross of her beloved and most perfect Son, who had taken on the sins of the world—including yours.

Read Luke 23:44–49, and read it a second time more slowly. Then read it for a third time, noting the words or thoughts that jump out at you.

> It was now about the sixth hour, and there was darkness over the land until the ninth hour, while the sun's light failed; and the curtain of the temple was torn in two. Then Jesus, crying with a loud voice, said, "Father, into thy hands I commit my spirit!" And having said this he breathed his last. Now when the centurion saw what had taken place, he praised God, and said, "Certainly this man was innocent!" And all the multitudes who assembled to see the sight, when they saw what had taken place, returned home beating their breasts. And all his acquaintances and the women who had followed him from Galilee stood at a distance and saw these things.

Now, ask yourself:

- What do I hear? (Write down the words or phrases that stand out to you as you read.)

- What does it mean? (Write down what you think about those words, or why you think they're important.)

- What is Jesus saying to me? (Write what you hear Jesus saying into your heart, and respond to him.)

Questions for Group Discussion
by Dr. Carol Younger

1. *Enter the Scripture.* Jesus is compassion and love itself, even on his way to crucifixion. He redirects the women following him from their mourning for himself to their compassion and consolation toward others. In the future, others will suffer in the fall of Jerusalem. His suffering is offered for those who have lost or will lose the life of grace because of sin. He asks the women to weep and pray for them, he says, not for himself.

    For what death, or for what loss of grace, do you mourn? A family member, a lost relationship, or someone's separation from the Church? Share that loss with its spiritual significance in your group. What compassion or consolation can you offer to the others you know who are affected by this same loss?

2. *Walk in Her Sandals.* Veronica's story begins "I shouldn't be here," and ends, "I am just where I should be." Many other ironies are in her story: comforting her son after his little fall to wiping the Son of Man when he falls; the care for her own little son to caring for Jesus' Mother; carrying bread to the poor of the city to finding the Bread of Life for the world; and wondering who Jesus really is to finding out who she herself really is, a disciple of the Son of God.

Who is Jesus to you in your life? Where is he, secretly or openly, in family, community, and spiritual life? How do you balance active charity with Eucharist and prayer? Asking Mary to help you see Jesus, share some smaller part of these answers.

3. *Unwrap the Gift.* Tradition tells us that no person, other than Jesus himself, suffered as much as his Mother, Mary, suffered at Calvary. At the foot of the cross, witnessing the evil of sin and the murder of her Son, and aware of the love of his Sacred Heart even for his executioners, her Immaculate Heart breaks. And she offers that heartbreak back to God with love for us in union with her Son.

What event of your life or person in your life caused your sensitive heart to break? If you are able, share what you can of that heartbreak. What memory of that hurt would you like to offer back to God now, in this moment, for the love of others in your life?

4. *Reflect on the Meaning.* As we saw in Laura's story about her son, Zach, a mother's urge to give life and protection to her child does not end when that child leaves her womb. Fetal cells multiply in the thousands, even millions, in the body of the pregnant woman. Even if the child has died, part of him lives on in the heart of the mother. And even after her death, part of her remains alive in him. The two share an inseparable bond, united on a cellular level.

If you have children, how do you experience this with them? For what aspects of your children's life and personalities are you grateful? How do you care for your children spiritually and emotionally when they are not by your side, away at school or activities, or have grown and married, or left home? What do you ask God for in their lives? Laura Sobiech asked God for Zach's life and death to be "for something big"—changing at least a single life.

How do you see your children changing others' lives, changing them for God?

The profound mystery of the connection between mother and child, on a cellular level, has implications for us as well when we consider the relationship between Jesus and the Blessed Mother. "From his conception onward, cells from Jesus . . . remained within Mary."[4] Think of it: when we are baptized, we are in Jesus. When we are in Jesus, we are in Mary. We are her children. She loves us and is grateful for our life in Christ!

As you go about your day, how often do you think of Mary and speak to her, as a daughter speaks to her mother? Which of her qualities do you most want to imitate?

Walking in the New Evangelization
by Kelly Wahlquist

As we conclude this chapter, think about what new insights or "God prompts" you have experienced as you reflected on the experiences of these women. Here are a couple of ways you can continue to reflect upon what you have discovered in the coming week!

Contemplate Your Own Gifts

"Passion" comes from the Greek word meaning "suffer." Whenever we suffer, we have the opportunity to participate in Christ's suffering and in his glory. In his book *When You Suffer*, Jeff Cavins says, "In human suffering there is an immeasurable treasure, and that treasure has the power to assist in the redemption of mankind."[5] Simply put, when united with Jesus' suffering, your suffering has tremendous meaning. Spend a few minutes each day this week reflecting on the blessings of the day and the sufferings offered to you. Choose a special person or intention each day for the gifts and another for the sufferings. Reflect on how that increases your sensitivity to the meaning of both the gift and the suffering.

Faith in Action

Go out of your way this week to alleviate the suffering of someone. It could be as simple as listening with your heart to someone you encounter, someone you do not already count as a friend. Or it could be as big as serving in a soup kitchen. It's up to you; challenge yourself to see others and stand with them in their suffering. At the end of the week, ask Mary to take your offering to Jesus.

4.

The Gift of Prayer

(Holy Saturday)

A Moment to Ponder
by Kelly Wahlquist

The catechism tells us that "the bodies of the dead must be treated with respect and charity, in faith and hope of the Resurrection" (*CCC*, 2300). In first-century Palestine, however, crucified criminals were seldom granted a dignified repose. Joseph of Arimathea, a secret believer, asked Pilate for the body of Jesus in order to give him a proper burial (see Mk 15:43). John tells us that Nicodemus also assisted (see Jn 19:39–40), but he does not say whether the Blessed Mother, Mary Magdalene, or the other women helped. (In this chapter each of the writers interprets this silence a bit differently.)

No doubt those who loved Jesus mourned his death; no doubt, their grief was manifested in prayer as they watched the cold, still body of the Lord carried to what they thought was his final resting place: prayers of anguish, prayers of trust, and prayers of hope. This gift of prayer, which consoles us even in the darkest moments of our lives, will be the focus of this chapter.

Enter the Scripture
by Sarah Christmyer

Scripture is nearly silent about Holy Saturday. It's as if, with the death of our Lord, everything stops. There is a flurry of preparation in the short time between his death and the start of the Sabbath: Joseph of Arimathea wraps the body of Jesus carefully and lays it in a new tomb not far from the cross. The women prepare aromatic oils and spices, but there is no time to anoint the body, and they retire to their homes. Meanwhile, the chief priests and Pharisees get Pilate to seal the tomb and mount a Roman guard. A profound silence begins.

It is a time of waiting and rest. How fitting it is that the Lord's death would usher in the Sabbath! God rested after his creative work; now Jesus rests after his redemptive work. The Father rests, the Son rests, and the world rests, and waits, for the revelation of redemption.

Luke punctuates the time between burial and resurrection with a single line: "On the sabbath they rested according to the commandment" (Lk 23:56). It is a pause pregnant with tension. "It is *not* finished" as far as anyone who lives is concerned.

We can imagine the Jewish leaders pacing in their robes, grimly glad to have seen the end of this rabble-rouser yet wondering if the disciples will make a move to steal the body. Will the guard hold? Will the man be made a martyr and ignite more discontent?

We can see the apostles cowering in a locked room. Their Lord was crucified. Will they be next? We can see the women hugging their shawls around themselves, absorbed in grief and painful questions even as they try to observe the Sabbath. We can imagine them checking the spices again and again, making sure there are enough. We can see them tossing in their beds and then waiting by the door ready to pick up those spices the moment the sky announces the end of the Sabbath. There will be no delay in caring for their beloved.

And Mary? Where is she? John tells us that from the hour of Jesus' death, he "took her to his own home" (Jn 19:27). We can see John, the disciple Jesus loved, and Mary, who undoubtedly loved Jesus more than life itself—two who were joined as family by Jesus' final act on the cross—observing that Sabbath together. I would like to have been the proverbial "fly on the wall" in John's house that day. When people love and are loved as those two were, what do the hours after the loved one's death look like?

Surely they mourned. That day was horrific, and they are human after all. Yet Mary has been formed by decades of pondering. God promised to give her a son who would be called the Son of the Most High and who would reign forever. God filled her empty womb with blazing life. She was warned that a sword would pierce her soul (see Lk 2:35). She knew her Son was to be "about his father's business." Surely she heard Jesus predict his death and resurrection. Surely she heard the report from Martha that Jesus raised Lazarus and said, "I am the resurrection and the life" (Jn 11:25).

Perhaps Mary repeats to John the words of Jesus: "With God, all things are possible" (Mt 19:26). Two thousand years earlier, an angel said those same words to Abraham and Sarah about another impossible child, who later had reason to ask, "Where is the lamb for a burnt offering?" (Gn 22:7). Abraham offered his promised son, knowing that God could raise him to life if necessary (see Heb 11:19). Did John and Mary think of that, and ponder?

For his part, John is "the beloved disciple" who rested on Jesus' breast at the Last Supper. He saw Jesus raise Jairus's young daughter to life (see Mk 5). He was an eyewitness of the Transfiguration and heard God say from the cloud, "This is my beloved Son" (Mt 3:17). He was with Jesus in his agony in the garden and was the only apostle who stayed by him to the end.

John and Mary do not seem to have been present when Joseph buried Jesus, and Mary doesn't seem to have taken part in preparing the spices. Perhaps they knew there was something deeper going on. They may have welcomed the Sabbath. It freed them from other obligations, allowed them to ponder together just what Jesus' death might mean. It would be natural for them to repeat and discuss his final words:

"Today you will be with me in Paradise" (Lk 23:43).

He said that to a thief! Was he, then, in paradise? Does his kingship involve bringing people there?

"Father, into thy hands I commit my spirit!" (Lk 23:46).

These words give no room for hatred or revenge against the authorities. Jesus offered his own life! Maybe John told Mary Jesus' words at the Last Supper: "This is my body which is given for you. . . . This cup which is poured out for you is the new covenant in my blood" (Lk 22:19–20). Maybe those cryptic words began to make sense. What they had witnessed was not an execution. It was a perfect sacrifice.

Maybe John shared with Mary other things Jesus said at the Last Supper, things he would later write in his gospel:

> Now I am going to him who sent me. . . . You will weep and lament, but the world will rejoice; you will be sorrowful, but your sorrow will turn into joy. When a woman is in travail she has sorrow, because her hour has come; but when she is delivered of the child, she no longer remembers the anguish, for joy that a child is born into the world. So you have sorrow now, but I will see you again and your hearts will rejoice, and no one will take your joy from you. . . . I have said this to you, that in me you may have peace. In the world you have tribulation; but be of good cheer, I have overcome the world. (Jn 16:5, 20–22, 33).

Did these things infuse their mourning with hope?

"It is finished," Jesus said before he died (Jn 19:30).

What is finished, the work Jesus came to do? His "hour"—like the hour of the woman in labor—had come. Hidden away in the womb of the tomb, new life was about to burst forth.

Scripture may be silent about the events of Holy Saturday, but the Church is not. Consider the words of this ancient homily, which is part of the Divine Office for Holy Saturday: "Something strange is happening—there is a great silence on earth today. . . . The earth trembled and is still because God has fallen asleep in the flesh and he has raised up all who have slept ever since the world began. God has died in the flesh and hell trembles with fear."

In a mother's womb, contractions precede the birth. At Christ's death, an earthquake opened graves and bodies were raised. Jesus, having conquered sin and death and the devil on the cross, descended into hell (Sheol) to release the holy souls who had died before him. "This is the day when our Savior broke through the gates of death!"[1]

Every Holy Saturday, the Church waits as it were beside the tomb, meditating on Christ's death while awaiting the announcement of his resurrection. Like John, we can take Mary into our homes and ponder with her the last words of Christ. Like her, we can rest in a place between anguish and joy, waiting in quiet hope. We can pray the Divine Office, which parts the veil to show us Christ defeating death and releasing sinners from captivity. The King is not dead; he rests from his work. A new day will come. His Cross is not defeat; it is victory!

Walk in Her Sandals: Zilpah's Story

by Stephanie Landsem

Silence.

Zilpah sat in the courtyard with Miriam, Huldah, Veronica, and Anah. Their weeping had ended, but tears had brought no solace. Their questions remained unanswered; their prayers, unheard. Only the stillness filled the void.

In her long years, Zilpah had known many kinds of silence: the unspoken contentment she felt as she worked alongside a dear friend; and sitting in stillness, lifting her heart in prayer without a word, yet knowing her God was present. She had known joyful silence, when she looked upon a newborn babe with no words to express the love in her heart. But this . . . this was the insidious silence of the enemy, stealing their hope, rending their souls, and replacing their joy with bitterness. This silence must be battled with prayer.

Anah slumped outside her door. Miriam and Huldah leaned together beneath the fig tree. They, along with Veronica, had stayed with Mary, the mother of Jesus, while she had seen the body of her son laid in the tomb and had only returned home as dusk fell on the beginning of the Sabbath.

Zilpah leaned against the cold bricks; the cooking fire crackling at her feet seemed to give off no heat. Her body ached—an ache deeper than muscle, deeper than bone. She closed her eyes. At her age, she sometimes couldn't recall what had happened days or even hours before. Yet memories of years past visited her often, like old friends. The first time she had seen the child, Jesus, was at least twenty years ago.

Mary had been young then, and her husband had been alive.

Zilpah had heard at the well that Mary of Nazareth was frantically searching Jerusalem for her missing child, a boy named Jesus. Zilpah had dropped her water jar and gone to find Mary, bringing her to the Temple, where she'd seen Jesus speaking with the rabbis like a man twice his age.

Pain pierced Zilpah's heart like an arrow. Even then, Jesus had been extraordinary.

She had listened, astonished at Jesus' words to his worried mother, "Did you not know I would be in my Father's house?" It was then she had realized Jesus was unlike other men; he was the one they had been awaiting.

Since then, Zilpah had waited and prayed. She waited for him to reveal himself. She prayed she would be ready—that they all would be ready. Now, the Messiah—Jesus, the boy she knew years ago—was dead.

This Sabbath morning, there was much to ponder in her heart and much she didn't understand. But she knew one thing, the man named Jesus had been sent by God. For what purpose and how his story would end, she did not know.

Last night, before the Sabbath began, Ephraim and Joses had gone to find James, to make sure he was safe. As twilight fell, Veronica and Anah had exchanged worried glances. As the night darkened, they began to pray. Late in the night, the men returned.

Anah and Veronica had run to their husbands in relief. Miriam asked, her voice breaking, "James . . . did you find him?"

Joses shook his head, his voice grim. "No. Jesus' followers, they've scattered. The authorities are looking for them." He went to his mother and put his arms around her. "I hope he left Jerusalem."

Now, as the dawn stained the sky in the east, Veronica, her eyes ringed with red, her hair uncovered and uncombed, came to Zilpah. In her hand, she had a folded head covering, the one she'd made just days before of fine white linen. As always, Veronica's beautiful face was easy to read, and Zilpah could see uncertainty along with her sorrow.

"What is it, my child?"

With shaking hands, Veronica unfolded the cloth. Zilpah's old heart pounded. Were her eyes deceiving her? With a bent, wrinkled finger she traced the likeness of a man, made in blood and dirt. "It is he."

Veronica nodded. In a halting whisper, she told Zilpah of how she found Jesus carrying his cross, of how she wiped his face and he gave her this gift. "Should I . . ." she swallowed and looked up at Zilpah. "Should I show it to Joses?"

Zilpah looked at this young girl, so hesitant and unsure. "You must decide, my dear," she said kindly. "You must decide if your love for your husband outweighs your fear of him." It was time—past time—for Veronica to become the wife Joses needed. But she would have to come to that decision herself. No one could do it for her.

Veronica bit her lip and looked again at the image of the man on the cloth, and then nodded and stood. She folded the cloth and went into the house where Joses slept.

The fire burned down to embers as Zilpah wondered at Veronica's revelation. The courtyard gate creaked. James, his clothes rumpled and his hair sticking up, pushed through it. He fell to his knees in front of his mother. Miriam put her arms around him. "James, thank the Most High." Anah stumbled across the courtyard and joined in the embrace.

"Mother," James voice cracked. He swallowed hard. "He's dead. Jesus . . ." He buried his face in her shoulder. "We thought . . . how could this happen?"

Veronica came from her house, followed by Joses. In one hand, she held the folded head covering; the other was grasped tightly by her husband. Joses's face was pale, and his eyes were fixed on his brother.

James stood unsteadily and faced his older brother. "Say it, then, Joses." His voice broke. "You were right, about Jesus; he wasn't who we thought he was."

Joses stepped toward his brother. Miriam and Anah stepped closer to James, as if to protect him from his brother's scorn. But instead of rebuke, Joses embraced his brother, kissing him on the cheek. "No, James," his deep voice held real anguish. "It is I who am sorry, for my stubbornness, my hardness of heart. I was wrong to call you a fool."

Miriam pulled Joses close, and Zilpah could see the glint of tears in Joses's eyes. She caught Veronica's glance, and the girl pressed the veil close to her heart. Praise the Most High. She doubted her stubborn grandson believed Jesus was sent by God, but the wall between Joses and James had cracked and—with the help of the Most High—perhaps would crumble.

James pulled back from his brother's embrace, his face still troubled. "But you were right about Jesus." James slumped back down on the ground. "And now he's dead."

Joses pulled his mother and brother close to the fire. He brought them both stools to sit on and sat next to them. "I think he was more than any of us realized." He signaled to Veronica, and she spread the veil over her lap. In a soft voice, encouraged by Joses, she related how she had seen Jesus. Miriam and Huldah exclaimed, running their fingers caressingly over the agonized face. Anah, too, drew close to examine it.

James still shook his head, "But now he is dead! We thought change was coming. But nothing has changed."

Zilpah felt a spark of anger. She hadn't raised her grandson to give up so easily. Where was his faith? Did it wither and die so quickly when tested? Perhaps it was time to remind them all of who Jesus was and what he had done. She took up a stick and stirred the fire until the flames blazed and sparks flew in the air. "James. Tell us about Lazarus."

"Lazarus." James stared into the flames as if he could see something within it no one else could see.

"Yes." Zilpah encouraged. "Tell us what happened."

Joses leaned in, his face open and curious. Veronica scooted closer to her husband. Anah brought a stool and settled next to them.

James sighed. "We were east of the river. He was teaching in the Greek cities. A man came and told us Lazarus was sick, dying. We expected Jesus to go to him. He is—was—a good friend of the family. But he didn't. We stayed for days. Then, we got word he was dead."

"And still Jesus went." Zilpah said, her heart quickening.

James nodded. "Yes. We went. And Martha met us outside the town. She said . . ." His brow pulled down in concentration.

"What did she say?" Anah urged.

"She said, 'I believe you are the one sent by God. Anything you ask, God will give you.'"

"And what did Jesus say?" Joses jumped in. He'd heard the story too; it was all around the city just days earlier. But he waited with expectation, as if hearing for the first time.

James rubbed his beard. "He said, 'Your brother will rise.'"

A shiver of anticipation went through Zilpah's old bones.

"What happened?" This was from Veronica, who clutched the cloth to her chest, her eyes wide.

"He wanted to go to the tomb." James's voice was flat and dull. "He called for them to roll the stone aside. And then . . ." James stared into the fire for a moment. "And then he said to Lazarus, 'Come out.' And he came out of his tomb. He was alive. No one could believe it."

Joses shook his head. "You saw this? You're sure?"

"Yes. With my own eyes. He was dead and then he was alive." He dropped his head in his hands, and his voice was anguished. "But don't you see? Now Jesus is dead. How can a dead man raise himself?"

Zilpah fought the urge to slap her grandson's thick skull. "You of little faith!" she sputtered, "It is easy to remain faithful when all is well; it is an act of true love to remain faithful when all seems to be lost."

James stared at her, his mouth open.

Zilpah took a deep breath and laid her wrinkled hand on James's cheek. "My boy, for thousands of years, we have waited and prayed for the Messiah. Martha and Mary waited, even though their brother was dead."

Miriam and Anah looked at her with understanding dawning in their eyes. Huldah leaned close, her broad face creased in concentration. Veronica looked at the veil in her lap, her finger tracing the line of Jesus' brow.

"Perhaps she's right," Joses's voice was soft, as if he were speaking to himself. He turned to James. "Perhaps this isn't the end of the story."

James stuttered, "But what are we to do now, with him gone?"

Zilpah's heart filled with the hope that had been absent since the darkness descended the day before. "We wait and we pray." Zilpah closed her eyes and began to sing in her quavering voice. Anah joined in, and then Miriam and Huldah.

> My spirit faints within me;
>> my heart within me is appalled.
> I remember the days of old,
>> I meditate on all that thou hast done;
>> I muse on what thy hands have wrought.

Joses, his hands clasped in Veronica's, added his deep voice to theirs.

> I stretch out my hands to thee;
>> My soul thirsts for thee like a parched land.
> Make haste to answer me, O Lord!
>> My spirit fails!

Finally, James's voice sounded with them, and the prayer filled the courtyard, banishing the despair and doubt that lingered in the shadows.

> Hide not thy face from me,
>> Lest I be like those who go down to the Pit.
> Let me hear in the morning of thy steadfast love,
>> For in thee I put my trust.

As the last words echoed across the wall, silence once again suffused the courtyard. But now, the bonds of brotherhood had been remade, and as they all joined together in prayer, faith in Jesus had been reborn. Zilpah felt the silence sink into her soul. No, this was not the silence of despair but of a burgeoning hope, a fragile, growing hope.

"For how long?" James asked his grandmother. "How long must we wait for the Lord to answer our prayer?"

"For as long as it takes," Zilpah answered. "Until the end of the story. Or until the beginning."

Unwrap the Gift of Prayer
by Pat Gohn

*How long have you waited with silent—or perhaps not-so-silent—
longing for the Lord to answer your prayer? The great mystery
that is at the heart of prayer lies at the crux of our free will and the
benevolent love of God, who deigns to work on our behalf (though
not always the way we expect). This willingness to embrace the mystery, and to continue to hope and trust in the goodness of the Lord,
is part of the unique feminine gift of prayer.* —Kelly Wahlquist

St. John Damascene taught, "Prayer is the raising of one's
mind and heart to God or the requesting of good things from
God" (*CCC*, 2590).

Prayer is a gift—and a discipline. It is a natural expression
of the gift of faith, an interior disposition, and a movement
of the heart. We were made for prayer and are hardwired
for God. "The desire for God is written in the human heart"
(*CCC*, 27).

God longs to draw us to himself through an ongoing
conversation with him. The catechism declares, "The life of
prayer is the habit of being in the presence of . . . God and in
communion with him" (*CCC*, 2565). Prayer is the habit of the
faithful woman. The feminine gifts we've already discussed—
receptivity, generosity, and sensitivity—help to shape a strong
and intimate prayer life.

The gift of *receptivity* helps us to receive God's love and
direction. It opens us to listen and contemplate and hold
God's goodness in our very depths.

Generosity inspires us to spend our love on God. A wise
spiritual director once advised, "Be generous with the Lord."
For me, that means making daily prayer a priority. It also
means lavishing my love on God by serving his people to the
best of my abilities.

The gift of *sensitivity* moves us to be intercessors in prayer.
Our prayers often take on a maternal care when we pray for

people and situations that require graces and a tender touch from God. We petition the Lord with the needs we hold in our hearts. We pray as Jesus did, asking things of our heavenly Father.

Today we consider this gift of prayer in light of the silence of Holy Saturday. In the Triduum timeline, it is the great waiting. Jesus is in the tomb. Back in the days of Christ and the first apostles, the great glory of the Resurrection was yet unknown, even though Jesus predicted it.

Holy Saturday was the Sabbath, a day of rest and of prayer for the Jewish community. It was also, for many acquainted with Jesus, a day of darkness due to the grief and sadness over his hideous death. And yet, for the observant Jews, the routine Sabbath rituals of prayer and remembrance provided a measure of comfort. Even in those dark moments, there is a Sabbath rest.

In times of trials, darkness, and sorrow, prayer reawakens the heart and the memory of God's good graces and stead-fast love. Prayer remembers that what God says is true and trustworthy. And we learn that trust by making it a habit to be in his presence. In the words Jesus spoke to Martha, "If you would believe you would see the glory of God" (Jn 11:40). Those words hold promise for us today as well.

As you come to Holy Saturday, consider the gift of prayer:

1. "Prayer is a gift and a discipline." In what ways have you experienced the truth of this statement?

2. One of the most important—and least understood—aspects of prayer is waiting. Can you think of a time when you waited (even impatiently) for God to answer your prayer and were surprised at the answer?

3. If God is omniscient and omnipotent—that is, he knows everything and has the power to accomplish anything—then why does he want us to pray?

Reflect on the Meaning: Holy Saturday
by Kelly Wahlquist

My prayers will probably never grace the pages of a spiritual self-help book or be posted on Pinterest in some flowery font, but I know God hears them. You see, my prayers are less than poetic, but they do come from the quiet, and sometimes chaotic, corners of my heart. No matter how jumbled my thoughts may be, the Lord understands and answers me. Many times his answers astonish me.

Take, for instance, the very concept of this book you are reading. One Good Friday after Communion, I was meditating on the meaning of this "horrible" day we call "good" when my thoughts were distracted. The choir was singing, "Stay with me . . . remain here with me . . . watch and pray . . . watch and pray." Suddenly my prayer went straight to God before I had time to filter it, and I said to him, "This is stupid. Why are we singing this song? This is so yesterday in the Garden of Gethsemane! Don't they know you are dead and buried now? Who would be watching and praying tonight?"

No sooner had the thought entered my mind than the Lord gave me the answer, and I responded, "Of course, you're right, Lord." Someone was watching and praying that first Holy Saturday. It was the same someone who did not sleep a wink even when the apostles lost the battle to keep their eyes open. She prayed unceasingly throughout the entire dreadful night, because she always does the will of God. That someone, of course, is Mary.

On that first Good Friday, from the cross, Jesus had given her to John, and to the world, to be our Mother. On that horrible night of unbearable suffering, Mary prayed for her sons and daughters, who must have believed their world was ending. And yet their perfect Mother watched over them and prayed with them.

At Cana, she had said, "Do whatever he tells you." At Calvary, she showed them with her own actions how to do what he told them to do—to watch and pray. She taught them to be patient in tribulation and constant in prayer.

Holy Saturday is a day when the earth waits in silence. It is a time suspended between two worlds: the death of Good Friday and the Resurrection of Easter. It's a moment balancing between sadness and joy. That concept of life hanging in the balance, of time being suspended, conjures up thoughts of another instance where we hear time stood still (in a manner of speaking). At the Annunciation all of heaven awaited the answer of a young woman from Nazareth. Reflecting on that concept in light of Holy Saturday brings a new understanding of what that time of waiting must have been like for Mary, the other women and disciples, and the apostles on that day of great silence more than two thousand years ago.

I've always seen that first Holy Saturday as a day filled with intense pain, with feelings of desolation, failure, and fear, and I imagined the prayers of those closest to Jesus were prayers of lamenting. Had I been there, I would have been crying out, "Be gracious to me, O LORD, for I am languishing; Oh LORD, heal me, for my bones are troubled. My soul also is sorely troubled. But thou, O LORD—how long?" (Ps 6:2–3). Actually, I probably would have said something more along the lines of, "Lord, I am broken, and I don't understand. Why, Lord, why? Why did you leave? What do I do now? Help me!"

But now, I no longer believe that the prayers on that first Holy Saturday were lamentations, because on that day, Mary, spiritual Mother to all, would have done what she had always done. She would have trusted in the will of God, pondered that which she could not completely comprehend, and prayed as she was taught and as was the custom of the Jewish people; in times of great unrest, confusion, or trial, Mary would be giving glory to God. Even in moments of silence, in her heart she would be glorifying God.

What a beautiful lesson our Blessed Mother teaches us about how to weather the "Holy Saturdays" of our lives, the times when we are teetering on despair. In the midst of great suffering and tribulation, we can and should turn to prayer, and our first prayer should be one of praise and thanksgiving. It sounds simple enough, but I know firsthand how difficult it can be to find words of praise in the dark moments of life. In times such as these, I turn to one whose words are much more poetic than mine. In moments when my world is suspended between joy and sadness, praying Psalm 113 turns my thoughts away from my own suffering and floods my soul with confidence and trust in God's goodness. I think this is what Holy Saturday is all about, being patient and always trusting in God's plan of sheer goodness, regardless of the depth of the darkness or the magnitude of the silence that surrounds us.

Ultimately, God is calling us every day to watch and pray, and knowing the end of the story, we can do this in hope and with great anticipation of the joy that awaits us. —Kelly Wahlquist

Lectio for Holy Saturday

Read John 19:40–42, and read it a second time more slowly. Then read it for a third time, noting the words or thoughts that jump out at you.

> They took the body of Jesus, and bound it in linen cloths with the spices, as is the burial custom of the Jews. Now in the place where he was crucified there was a garden, and in the garden a new tomb where no one had ever been laid. So because of the Jewish day of Preparation, as the tomb was close at hand, they laid Jesus there.

Now, ask yourself:

- What do I hear? (Write down the words or phrases that stand out to you as you read.)

- What does it mean? (Write down what you think about those words, or why you think they're important.)

- What is Jesus saying to me? (Write what you hear Jesus saying into your heart, and respond to him.)

Questions for Group Discussion
by Dr. Carol Younger

1. *Enter the Scripture.* By instituting the Eucharist at that Last Supper, not only does Jesus change the way Passover is celebrated, but also his passion changes our perception of both sin and death. From the cross he forgives sins: "This day you will be with me in Paradise." Though it was likely not apparent to those who watched the crucifixion, for us the Cross is a sign of triumph and hope. Holy Saturday, then, is about more than the commandment to rest on the Sabbath. It is about resting in hope and prayer, knowing that Christ has won for us victory even over death.

    For what victory over death do you pray on this Holy Saturday? Are you praying for a friend or relative who has distanced him- or herself from the sacramental life of the Church? Are you praying for your own victory over a threat to your relationship with Jesus, or for the release of holy souls from purgatory.

2. *Walk in Her Sandals.* At the beginning, Zilpah, overcome with sadness at Jesus' death, cannot even pray in the silence. However, when confronted with the despair of James and others, she rises from her own sorrow and becomes a prophetess. As she hears Lazarus's story again, it is she who speaks aloud the need for prayer and faithful waiting to the disciples of Jesus. It is in the story of Jesus' power over death that we are able to pray in the silence of our own sorrows. When, in the face of terminal illness, death, loss of significant safety, or the dimming of

future hopes and dreams, have you been tempted to stay in silence and sorrow, unable to pray? Can you share that situation and your sense of hopelessness at that time? How were you "raised" from that hopelessness? Please share that hope.

3.   *Unwrap the Gift.* Sabbath rest physically expresses trust in God. God might work on Sabbath keeping the crops growing and the world turning, but the heart of the faithful Jew rested in God and let him take care of today and tomorrow. After the crucifixion of Jesus, the apostles' Sabbath trust must have been difficult. Habit and practiced prayer must have taken over, in spite of their fright and despondency. When has habit or memorized prayer "saved" you from paralyzing fear or despair? Maybe you turned to rosary beads and recited prayers, or maybe you went straight to the Tabernacle and poured out your heart, asking for help. Share that time of suffering or sorrow and the prayer practice that lifted your heart and mind to God.

4.   *Reflect on the Meaning.* Mary's faith on Holy Saturday is expressed in her trust and her silence. On that dark evening, the apostles and many others who had followed Jesus would not find rest, and the wait for morning would seem impossibly long. For Mary, it was another "in-between time." There was the time between the Annunciation and the birth, the in-between discovery of loss and the finding of Jesus in the Temple, and the in-between time of the request and wine in the jars at Cana. Now, they faced the in-between time of the burial and whatever comes next. Is there an in-between time in your life, which you can share? Choose any of the above in-between moments of Mary to reflect on, and recall an event in your life when your trust filled the in-between time.

Walking in the New Evangelization
by *Kelly Wahlquist*

As we conclude this chapter, think about what new insights or "God prompts" you have experienced as you reflected on the experiences of these women. Here are a couple of ways you can continue to reflect upon what you have discovered in the coming week.

Contemplate Your Own Gifts

Set aside an hour to be with Jesus. Either go to a church to pray or sit in a quiet corner of your home. Write on a small pad the names of friends and family members who have died. Recall them one at a time, remembering their mannerisms and how they looked. Say a prayer of your choice, spontaneous or from a book or the Bible. Offer that prayer for their souls to be united with Jesus in victory over death. Close your time with Jesus by thanking him for putting these people in your life.

Faith in Action

Choose a corporal work of mercy that suits your spirituality and gifts. Investigate the works of mercy provided by your parish. Choose one of those works of mercy, and volunteer in your parish for a couple of hours. Precede those hours with an hour of Eucharistic adoration, praying for those you will serve.

The corporal works of mercy are as follows:

1. Feed the hungry.
2. Give drink to the thirsty.
3. Clothe the naked.
4. Shelter the homeless.
5. Visit those in prison.
6. Comfort the sick.
7. Bury the dead.

5.

The Gift of Maternity

(Easter Sunday)

A Moment to Ponder

by Kelly Wahlquist

For some, the Light of the world falls upon the shadows very slowly, like a sunrise that sends its first tentative rays upon the horizon, warming the air with golden promise. For others, the light from the paschal candle is passed from one hand to the next, one candle to the next, until the entire sanctuary blazes with joy as the priest intones,

> Christ yesterday and today,
> the beginning and the end,
> Alpha and Omega,
> All time belongs to him,
> And all ages;
> To him be glory and power
> Through every age and forever. . . .
> By his holy and glorious wounds,
> May Christ our Lord guard and keep us. Amen.

This burst of light and joy is especially powerful for those who have known the anguish of hopes deferred and delayed.

And yet, even that unrequited longing is an expression of the gift, for it points to a greater purpose in store for all of us. In this chapter we will look at the reactions of those who received the fulfillment of their greatest desires and how the feminine gift of maternity played out for those who first laid eyes on the risen Christ.

Enter the Scripture
by Sarah Christmyer

This week we are delving into the scripture passages concerning the women and others at the tomb (Mt 28:1–15); the miracle of the empty tomb (Mk 16:1–13, Lk 24:1–12; Jn 20:1–10); and the appearance of the Lord to Mary Magdalene (Jn 20:11–18).

Easter means "East." To people who look to the sky for time and direction, east is the place of the sunrise. In this case, it announces the Son-rise.

On the third day after his death and burial, Jesus was raised bodily from the tomb. His resurrection lit up the world like the sun. As John wrote in the introduction to his gospel, his "life was the light of men. The light shines in the darkness, and the darkness has not overcome it" (Jn 1:4–5). John had seen the darkness, and now he saw the light. The fact that the Lord was not dead but had risen dawned gradually on his followers in the same five stages with which the sun greets a new day:

Stage One: First comes a change in the sky. The darkness washes slowly away in the light of the approaching rays. While it is still dark, the women bundle up their spices and ointments and go to the tomb to anoint Jesus' body. But neither death nor the stone, the seal, or the guard has been able to keep him there. Jesus is gone! It is the first hint of dawn. But what does it mean? They can only wonder. Mary Magdalene rushes to the disciples. "They have taken the Lord out of the tomb, and we do not know where they have laid him" (Jn 20:2).

Stage Two: Dawn arrives, and the world becomes visible yet is still in shadows. Peter and John race to the tomb, only to find it empty. Looking in, they see something Mary Magdalene missed. No thief has tampered with the tomb. The linen shroud lies deflated, as though Jesus simply rose out of it. The cloth that covered Jesus' face remains rolled and set apart from the rest. Someone raised like Lazarus would have unwrapped the clothes. Thieves would have stolen the cloths and left the body. But even if they wanted Jesus, what thief would strip the body before carrying it, let alone arrange the cloths to look as though they hadn't been touched?

John sees the empty shroud and believes. Faith precedes understanding.

Stage Three: Then light breaks over the horizon, illuminating the world. Peter and John return home, but Mary Magdalene stays weeping outside the tomb. "They have taken away my Lord," she says again—this time to an angel—"and I do not know where they have laid him" (Jn 20:13). Human sight keeps her from recognizing him when he appears behind her, but then he speaks into her grief. Jesus calls her by name, and with that personal touch, she sees. She clings to him. Maybe she's afraid he will leave. But he gives her something to do. I must ascend "to my Father and your Father," he says (Jn 20:17). *Our* Father, who art in heaven. Go; tell the others. "I have seen the Lord!" she tells them. She becomes an "apostle to the apostles," as she was referred to in early Christian writings.[1] She is the one who brings them the good news of the Resurrection.

Stage Four: Finally, the sun rises and can be seen in the sky. The apostles are hiding behind locked doors. They have seen their Lord crucified, and their grief has been upstaged by fear. The Sabbath is past. Will the authorities take action now against them?

Jesus appears among them. His body is recognizable but different. Locked doors cannot keep him out. There are holes in his hands and feet and a lance mark in his side. This is the crucified Jesus, but he is very much alive in a new and risen way. Those marks of death show that death has no hold on him. "Mary," he'd said to the Magdalene. But fear needs different words. "Peace be with you," he says to the apostles. Then he shows them his wounds, fatal yet somehow swallowed in life. "Peace be with you. As the Father has sent me, even so I send you" (Jn 20:21). Like Mary, they are given something to do. Is he sending them potentially to death also, yet to a new life regardless? "Receive the Holy Spirit," and forgive, he adds (Jn 20:22–23). The kingdom of this King will not be about taking revenge or strong-arming others. With peace and forgiveness it will continue to scatter the dark.

Stage Five: As the sun warms the earth, its heat can be felt. Eight days later, it is another first day of the week. It is the day of Resurrection that, for Christians, will replace the Sabbath. Thomas, who missed the earlier appearance of Jesus, doubts that he lives. Again Jesus appears through closed doors, and this time, he invites Thomas to put his fingers and hands in his wounds. Mary Magdalene heard, the other disciples saw, and now Thomas feels the Lord. "My Lord and my God!" he proclaims (Jn 20:28).

"Have you believed me because you have seen me?" Jesus asks. "Blessed are those who have not seen and yet believe" (Jn 20:29). That includes us!

"These [signs] are written that you may believe . . . and . . . have life in his name," John concludes (Jn 20:31). Perhaps you, yourself, are "dead" in some way. Jesus came that you might have life. "Once you were darkness, but now you are light in the Lord," St. Paul wrote to the Ephesians. "Awake, O sleeper, and arise from the dead, and Christ shall give you light" (Eph 5:14).

The Easter Vigil begins with a Service of Light. A fire is kindled outside of the church, in which people wait in darkness. Lighting the paschal candle from the new fire, the priest asks that the light of Christ, rising in glory, might "dispel the darkness of our hearts and minds." One by one, candles are lit from the paschal candle, until tiny flames fill the church. Then the Exsultet is sung. The whole story of salvation is proclaimed in this beautiful hymn.

Listen, and sing the words with a grateful heart of love:

> Let all corners of the earth be glad, knowing an end to gloom of darkness. Rejoice, let Mother Church also rejoice, arrayed with the lightning of his glory, let this holy building shake with joy.

Walk in Her Sandals: Miriam's Story
by Stephanie Landsem

Dark shadows clung to the corners and lingered in the alleys of Jerusalem as Miriam followed Mary Magdalene through the damp chill of predawn. Her feet were as heavy as millstones, her eyes gritty from countless tears and little sleep. The jar of myrrh weighed heavier in her hands with each step along the path of suffering Jesus had taken to Golgotha three days ago.

Her mother's song ebbed and flowed through her mind. *Do not hide your face from me, lest I become like those descending into the pit. At dawn let me hear your kindness, for in you I trust.*

The prayer soothed her aching soul, yet the underlying grief remained. Jesus was gone. The man she had served and loved, who had filled her heart with joy. She would no longer hear his voice or see his smile. He wouldn't call her "the other Mary" or laugh when James teased her. The year she had followed him with James was as a dream; and the last days here in Jerusalem, a nightmare.

Miriam and Mary Magdalene slipped out the Gennath Gate, not speaking to the keeper. Shepherds, wrapped in cloaks against the night chill, didn't raise their heads as the two women passed them by. No wind stirred the yellow blossoms of the mustard bushes or carried the scent of terebinth trees. No birdsong broke the silence. Stars glowed dimly in the cloudless western sky, even as the strands of red and amber colored the eastern horizon as rich and vibrant as silks from the Orient.

She had listened to Jesus' words, seen the miracles, and been filled with the belief that he was the one they had been waiting for. They had often spoken among themselves—she and Mary Magdalene, Joanna, and the other women—wondering what Jesus would do. But no one could have imagined he would leave them abandoned in Jerusalem, like a family without a father.

Wait and pray, Zilpah had said. Miriam rubbed a hand over her tired eyes. Wasn't it always such in the life of a woman . . . of a mother? Waiting and praying. Waiting for the flutter of new life in the womb and then for a child to be born. Praying for that child all the days of his or her life, be they short or long. She recalled the days carrying Joses, her first child. As her labor began, she had realized this pain of birth was the beginning of a new life—not only for her child but also for herself.

If this pain—this agony—of Jesus' death was indeed not the end but a beginning as her ancient mother promised, when would the beginning begin? *How long, O Lord, will we wait for your answer?*

Too soon, they were at the place of sorrow—Golgotha—the wretched site where their Lord had died. Miriam fell to her knees and bowed her head. Mary Magdalene knelt beside her. The sun broke over the horizon, dazzling their eyes with gold as pure as any king's treasure. Miriam's heart twisted at remembrance of the scene: Jesus, torn and bleeding, his lifeless body taken down from the cross and given to Mary, as an infant is laid in his mother's arms. Mary, her sorrow too deep for tears, had held him for the last time.

Miriam's dark thoughts grasped at happier memories. "Do you remember that night when we talked to Mary? After he raised Lazarus?" The day Lazarus had been raised was one of wonder and rejoicing. All of Bethany had gathered at the home of Martha, singing and praising God, everyone wanting to be close to Jesus, to touch Lazarus. Late that night, Miriam had gone with the other women in search of Mary, Jesus' mother. They found her alone in Martha's garden, prostrate in prayer. She knew that her son's time was approaching, even then. The women had stayed with Mary through the night, praying with her. As dawn broke that morning, Mary had told them of the angel who had come to her so many years before.

"Do not be afraid, he said to me," Mary had recounted in her gentle voice. "But I was. I was so very afraid of his light, the glory and brightness and beauty of him. And of what he asked of me. I knew it was my choice. To say no or to say yes. And my life would never be the same." Of course, she had said yes.

Miriam and Mary Magdalene had listened in wonder as Mary told the rest of the story: about Joseph, his dream, and how they had traveled to Bethlehem; and about the birth of the child and the angels and the shepherds. "He was never mine. He was the Lord's. But just in that moment, that first moment when I held him in my arms, he was my babe. And it was the greatest joy and I had ever known."

Now at another—more sorrowful—dawn, Miriam pushed herself to her feet and helped Mary Magdalene to stand. Jesus' burial on the eve of the Sabbath had been hurried, but today, with Miriam's myrrh and the aloes and spices Mary Magdalene had brought, they would anoint Jesus and say their last farewell.

Nearby lay the garden where Joseph of Arimathea had his tomb. It was an oasis of green amid the dry stones outside the city. As they drew closer, Miriam's grief turned to alarm. The garden was not deserted, as they had expected. Two Roman soldiers stood in front of the tomb, their armor glinting in the new rays of morning. Across the stone rolled over the opening of the tomb was the governor's seal.

Soldiers. When had they come? The Sanhedrin must have insisted on a guard and the royal seal. But how would they convince them to let them into the tomb? And who would roll the stone aside? *Lord be our help.*

Mary Magdalene glanced over at Miriam, squared her shoulders and walked purposefully down the path. Miriam had seen her deal with Romans before. If anyone could influence the guards, it would be Mary Magdalene, with her regal beauty and imperious manner.

"Stay back!" The guard closest to the tomb called out in thickly accented Greek. "No one may come here."

"We come only to—" Mary Magdalene's words were cut short as she stumbled. A sound like thunder seemed to come from the earth below their feet. Miriam clutched at Mary Magdalene as the ground moved under her. Rocks tumbled, breaking loose as the hillside pitched and buckled.

The Romans cried out in their own language, staggered, and fell to the ground as if struck by lightning.

"What is it?" Mary Magdalene held Miriam's arm in a desperate grip.

Miriam couldn't speak. A great light, so much brighter than the sun and more dazzling than gold, shone in front of the tomb, as if a star had come from the heavens down to earth. She shielded her eyes with her hand. A silence fell, except for the sound of stone scraping on stone.

Miriam lowered her hand from her eyes. Her legs weakened as though they were made of melting wax. The stone had rolled to the side, and a bright figure stood in front of the black opening. The presence—neither man nor woman but beautiful beyond expression—glowed as white as the snow on a mountaintop.

"Do not be afraid." The voice was like the chime of a thousand harps. "I know you are seeking Jesus the crucified." Next to her, Mary Magdalene gasped. Miriam's heart pounded in her ears, and her breath stopped in her throat.

The angel went on. "He is not here, for he has been raised. Just as he said."

Not here? Then where? And yet the rest of what the angel said—raised?—she could hardly grasp his meaning. Where could he be? She had seen his lifeless body put in the tomb.

"Come," the angel said with a voice like a ringing bell. "See the place where he lay."

Miriam took a step forward on trembling legs. Mary Magdalene held her hand in a grip so tight it hurt. Miriam's mouth was as dry as a broken pot, and just as unable to speak. The dazzling figure moved from the opening, and they looked in.

The tomb was empty.

The linen cloths that had wrapped their beloved teacher lay on the burial stone, flattened like empty wineskins, as if the body inside them had simply disappeared. Miriam heard a choked sob, a cry of disbelief. It had come from her own throat. Beside her, Mary Magdalene made no sound.

The voice of the angel sounded again, like a trumpet's call. "Go quickly and tell his disciples. Tell them, 'He has been raised from the dead, and he is going before you to Galilee; you will see him there.'"

Miriam looked at Mary Magdalene, whose face reflected her own dumbfounded amazement. Raised from the dead? Go to Galilee?

"Behold, I have told you," the angel declared, before glowing even more brightly and then vanishing from their sight.

The quiet he left behind was broken by a chorus of birds, the chirping of insects, and the song of the wind rushing through the trees, as if all of nature rejoiced.

Miriam and Mary Magdalene stood as still as statues.

One of the guards stirred, rolling over. Miriam forced herself to take a step back from the tomb. The other soldier groaned. She took Mary Magdalene's hand and pulled her away. "Hurry, before they wake."

They ran to the outskirts of the garden before Miriam stopped and turned. The open tomb, the guards lying on the ground . . . she hadn't imagined it. Miriam willed her legs to stop shaking. An angel, they had seen an angel. Who would believe them? Peter? James? No, they would scoff, even at Mary Magdalene. For why would an angel come to women? "What should we do?" she gasped.

Mary Magdalene looked around them, her breath coming fast. "Perhaps the gardener . . . ?" She motioned toward a man standing beside a copse of cedar trees.

Miriam followed her gaze. Where had he been when they arrived? He seemed to be waiting for something, watching them. Mary Magdalene approached him. "Sir, if you have carried him away, tell me, where?"

"Mary," the man said. As he spoke the word, it was if the light had fallen upon him and illuminated his face for her to see. Miriam's breath stopped in her throat. This man was no stranger—it was Jesus!

Mary Magdalene cried out—a joyful, surprised cry—and fell to her knees. "Rabbouni!"

Miriam dropped to her knees, her hands reaching out toward him, her joy leaping ahead of her thoughts. Jesus! He was alive. How could he be alive? The man she served, the rabbi she loved. Not dead but alive.

They reached out to him, touching feet that bore the gaping wounds where the nails had pierced them. Miriam's tears blurred her vision as Jesus lifted them up to stand in front of him. He shone with the dazzling light they had seen radiating from the angel.

"Do not be afraid," he told them in the same kind voice they had heard when they had served him. "Do not hold on to me, but go. Tell my brothers I am going to my Father and your Father, to my God and your God."

Miriam leaned toward him, a thousand questions tumbling within, but suddenly he was gone. She and Mary Magdalene stood alone, with the song of the birds in their ears, the wind whispering in the trees, and the city of Jerusalem spread out before them.

"I have seen the Lord." Mary Magdalene whispered, her hand over her heart.

A fierce joy seized Miriam as she finally realized. "He is alive!" She grabbed Miriam's shoulders. He was here before them and then gone. But not gone forever.

"We'll see him again in Galilee." Mary Magdalene's smile broke like the dawn.

"How can it be? What will they say?" They had been trusted to take the news to all who would listen. But would they listen?

"The men . . ." Magdalene's face clouded.

The men wouldn't believe them. At least not at first. But soon they would see and believe. This, then, was the beginning. The beginning of the beginning.

"Come," Miriam held out her hand. "We'll go. We'll announce the news to all who have ears to hear. He is risen!" Miriam linked her hand with Mary Magdalene's, and they began to run. Her legs were strong and as swift as a gazelle; her heart soared within her like a bird set free of its cage. Her soul kindled with the fire of love for her friend, her Messiah, her King.

Thank the Lord, oh my soul. The Lord had indeed answered her prayer. They would wait no more. A new life had begun on this day. The darkness had been overcome—transformed into bright, unfathomable light.

As they bounded toward the city, Mary Magdalene sang out the news, proclaiming for all to hear, "He is risen. Jesus is risen!"

And Miriam answered, her spirit rejoicing in the Lord, "Alleluia! Alleluia! He is risen, indeed."

Unwrap the Gift of Maternity
by Pat Gohn

Does it seem strange to you that this encounter at the tomb, at which Jesus' Mother is not present, is associated with the feminine gift of maternity? Think about it: not every woman will bear a child in her womb over the course of her lifetime, and yet every woman, by virtue of who she is, is called to carry life! In this story, the women at the tomb were entrusted with bringing the resurrected life of Jesus to his disciples. And in a special way, we are also called to imitate our Blessed Mother by carrying the life of Christ to the world around us. In this chapter, let's consider how we might do this! —Kelly Wahlquist*

Maternity doesn't just *rhyme* with eternity. It is *linked* to eternity. Through the gift of maternity women cooperate and cocreate with God. Regardless of their vocations, women are called to birth and nurture, either physically or spiritually, new lives that will live forever. Think of it: every human person who comes into existence in the womb of a woman, or who is nurtured by virtue of her loving heart, is destined to live forever. The ultimate goal of every life is new life in heaven.

God entrusts these new lives to women by virtue of their physical and spiritual motherhood, according to St. John Paul II: "The moral and spiritual strength of a woman is joined to her awareness that God entrusts the human being to her in a special way . . . precisely by reason of . . . femininity."[2]

Most of us understand the idea of becoming a mother and raising children. But many of us do not comprehend maternity's profound spiritual component. Although many women are called to give birth and raise families, *all* women are called to spiritual motherhood.

In the sacrament of Baptism, *godmothers* stand up for the newly baptized and assist the parents in nurturing the child's spiritual development. In the *religious life* of sisters and nuns, their spiritual union with Christ bears fruit through their spiritual maternity as they bring forth spiritual "children" through their apostolates of prayer and the works of mercy. Finally, the most extraordinary example of spiritual motherhood is the Blessed Mother, our mother in the order of grace. As we imitate her maternal goodness, our own souls will grow in beauty and goodness, bearing testimony of the love of God to everyone we encounter.

Let us consider the gift of maternity in light of Easter and the resurrection of Jesus. Actually, they both explain the gift of new life and the destiny of eternity. Human life cannot reach its divine end without the grace and power of the risen Lord.

Easter joy is the glory of God raising up the dead and broken Body of Christ. Not just a resuscitated body, this is a new, glorified, risen one. This new life in Christ also opens the doors of heaven that were closed due to sin. Thanks to Jesus' resurrection, and the merits of Baptism, every person who comes into existence has the potential for living his or her eternity in heaven. But first, God needs women to bring forth and nurture those souls.

Just as a soul bursts forth from the womb to begin a new life full of possibilities in its mortal life, Jesus' resurrection overcomes the tomb and offers us all a new life full of possibilities. Jesus offers us immortal life—the opportunity to become a child of God and a citizen of heaven.

As you come to Easter Sunday, consider your gift of maternity:

1. Have you ever considered the fact of your being a woman as a source of strength? In what ways?

2. Talk about the women who have been spiritual mothers to you. How did they share their feminine gifts with you?

3. What "spiritual children" has God placed in your path, and how are you going to nurture those lives for the glory of God?

Reflect on the Meaning: Easter Sunday
by Kitty Cleveland

"The Cross only makes sense in light of the Resurrection," my mother reminded me. As I pondered these words, it helped make sense of the suffering in my life, especially as it related to motherhood.

I grew up as the oldest of six girls, and I'd always just assumed I would have a large family with a guy who wanted just as many kids as I did. When I started dating Mel, it was simply because I found him handsome and interesting, not because he was marriage material. He was divorced with two children, was not a practicing Catholic, and was sixteen years my senior. He also didn't want to get married again and had ensured through a vasectomy that he would not father any more children. But he was lots of fun, was willing to have a (much-needed) wardrobe makeover, and did an excellent job of distracting me from my unhappiness working as a lawyer.

After a few months I was completely smitten and couldn't imagine my life without him. The feeling was clearly mutual when he offered to have the vasectomy reversed so that we could marry and have children together. We were engaged less than three months after our first date and married the following year, after Mel's annulment, in the beautiful St. Louis Cathedral in the heart of New Orleans. I instantly became a stepmother to two young teenagers. While the stepparenting classes I took before we married were helpful, there was only so much a class could teach. The next several years "grew me up" as I learned what real love required.

Sadly, the vasectomy reversal was a failure, and a second truly heroic reversal was also unsuccessful. I was heartbroken. In our desperation we even considered sperm aspiration and in vitro fertilization (IVF), until I received a phone call from a nun (tipped off by my concerned sister) who informed me that IVF was immoral.

"How can bringing new life into a loving marriage be wrong?" I asked incredulously. After all, I knew beautiful families who had children conceived in this way, and I didn't understand why we couldn't be one of them. She mentioned something about the moral necessity of both the unitive (physically joining man and woman) and procreative (being open to life) aspects of the marital act being present when new life is conceived, but this meant nothing to me. All I heard was that the Catholic Church was preventing us from having a baby, and I was heartbroken.

After months of grieving, I sat on my sofa and sobbed, "Lord Jesus, if this is really what you are asking of me—to sacrifice my unborn children—then I trust you. But please let me know if this is not your will!" Notwithstanding the anguish and the lack of understanding, there was now a supernatural peace in the middle of it that confirmed my decision. Surprisingly, my love for the Lord Jesus grew exponentially as this cross helped me to grow in intimacy with him.

My former pick-and-choose Catholicism according to the Church of Me had only brought confusion and lukewarmness of heart. And while this choice to follow authentic Church teaching was initially painful, I was ultimately given the grace I needed to accept with joy and gratitude this renunciation of my own will out of obedience, trust, and love. By trusting God and obeying the teachings of the Church, I experienced true freedom.

My hopes for motherhood were rekindled in 2003 when Mel and I were presented with the opportunity to adopt three frozen embryos from an acquaintance named Cecilia, a beautiful young mother of triplets and identical twins who had done IVF and was now dying of pancreatic cancer at the age of thirty-eight.

After much prayer and spiritual direction, we formally adopted these three little ones with the intent of implanting them in my womb and raising them as our own children. This gave Cecilia a great deal of peace as she prepared for her imminent death, and it gave me tremendous joy to collaborate with her in this unexpected way. I planned, God willing, to name one of my future daughters after her and St. Cecilia, patron saint of musicians.

When the day finally arrived for implantation, just weeks after Cecilia's funeral, all three of the embryos died in the thaw. I was crushed and, honestly, felt tricked by God. "Did I misunderstand you, Lord?" I sobbed. "Why did you let this happen?" Clearly, God's ways are not our ways.

Some months after Cecilia and the embryos died, I was praying in the adoration chapel when a woman approached and asked to speak to me outside. She wanted me to pray for her sixteen-year-old niece, who was pregnant and in a home for unwed mothers. "Does she have an adoptive family yet?" I asked tentatively. She did not, but she was interviewing them now. My heart began to pound when she introduced herself: "My name is Cecilia."

I rambled out the story about my friend and the frozen embryos, and how I wanted to name my little girl Cecilia. Her eyes widened as she said, "You won't believe it, but my niece has already named the baby Cecilia, after me." We both teared up as I thought, *This is my baby!*

Arrangements were made for my mom and me to drive up to Alabama to meet with the young mother and anxious grandmother. We spent hours with them, and I shared with the teenage mother my deep longing for a child. She shared her hopes for little Cecilia's future, and my mother reassured the grandmother that all would be well.

A few weeks later I got the grandmother's phone call: her daughter had chosen another family. My heart broke again, and though I knew God would never trick or abandon me, it certainly felt that way.

I have since come to understand that our sufferings are often an atonement for the sins of others—a participation in the priesthood of Christ conferred upon us in Baptism. This gives a redemptive meaning to the crosses we carry that I find deeply consoling.

After two more years—and a full twelve years after Mel and I married—God led us to adopt a beautiful baby girl from China, a precious sixteen-month-old whom we named, of course, Cecilia. After so many disappointments, God had at last granted me my heart's desire. I had become a mother—and to a child who would bring more love and joy to our family than I could have ever hoped for. It was a true match made in heaven.

Every year on July 20, our "Gotcha Day," I post a video of her toddling toward me between the beds in the hotel room while I cheer her on: "Come on! *You* can do it!" And when she finally makes it to me, I toss her in the air with boundless joy and then hold her tight, covering her in kisses. "I've got you! I've got you." Truly, the Cross only makes sense in light of the Resurrection.

Have you ever known someone who has struggled with issues of fertility, perhaps fearful of surrendering her fertility to God rather than controlling it through contraception on one hand or reproductive technologies on the other? Perhaps in no other area of life does the evil one work so hard to rob us of the giftedness that is ours in that surrender! If this is an issue for you, ask the Lord to transform you and your husband from the inside out, helping the two of you to come to a deeper understanding of his plan for your family. Consider making an appointment with your priest or spiritual director to help you. —Kelly Wahlquist

Lectio for Easter Sunday

Read John 20:11–18, and read it a second time more slowly. Then read it for a third time, noting the words or thoughts that jump out at you.

> But Mary stood weeping outside the tomb, and as she
> wept she stooped to look into the tomb; and she saw

two angels in white, sitting where the body of Jesus had lain, one at the head and one at the feet. They said to her, "Woman, why are you weeping?" She said to them, "Because they have taken away my Lord, and I do not know where they have laid him." Saying this, she turned round and saw Jesus standing, but she did not know that it was Jesus. Jesus said to her, "Woman, why are you weeping? Whom do you seek?" Supposing him to be the gardener, she said to him, "Sir, if you have carried him away, tell me where you have laid him, and I will take him away." Jesus said to her, "Mary." She turned and said to him in Hebrew, "Rab-boni!" (which means Teacher). Jesus said to her, "Do not hold me, for I have not yet ascended to the Father; but go to my brethren and say to them, I am ascending to my Father and your Father, to my God and your God." Mary Magdalene went and said to the disciples, "I have seen the Lord"; and she told them that he had said these things to her.

Now, ask yourself:

- What do I hear? (Write down the words or phrases that stand out to you as you read.)

- What does it mean? (Write down what you think about those words, or why you think they're important.)

- What is Jesus saying to me? (Write what you hear Jesus saying into your heart, and respond to him.)

Questions for Group Discussion
by Dr. Carol Younger

1. *Enter the Scripture.* Morning experiences can stay with us all day and into the evening. The early light and slow, soothing warmth assures us of the promise of a new day. No darkness can harm us; we've seen the sunrise and know it will return. Take some time and recall some things that happened in the morning during your life:

perhaps a special birthday when the family awakened you, getting up early for a hike or a fishing trip, the birth of your child, an early morning Mass at a small parish, or an early phone call. Choose one recollection, and share how it has stayed with you in memory. Think how it can be seen as a metaphor of your prayer life with Jesus.

2.   *Walk in Her Sandals.* Often, like Miriam, we stumble through experiences of darkness, carrying myrrh to anoint and bury some dream that has surely died. It only needs our letting go of the loss; then we can move on, slowly but resolutely. Maybe there is something in your life you struggle giving over to God. Perhaps you just bury it, busy yourself with some other thing, and move on resolutely. Then suddenly, God turns it all back around. The thing given up becomes a *new* thing, filled with joy and purpose. Share the memory of something given up, transformed by God, and given back to you, all new and filled with joy.

3.   *Unwrap the Gift.* Maternity is just the beginning of human life. Ask any mother. The day the baby comes home is the day she realizes the baby depends on *her*! It's the realization that this relationship is longer than life itself; the mother-and-child connection won't ever end, even after death. This is the same relationship God wants with us. Baptism begins that God-and-child eternal relationship. What do you know about your baptismal day, or the baptismal day of your children or godchildren? What do you know about your godmother? Are you a godmother? Share what you know about a baptismal day that told you of God's eternal love.

4.   *Reflect on the Meaning.* Speaking on the role of women, Pope Francis said, "Many things can change and have changed in cultural and social evolution, but there remains the fact that it is the woman who conceives, carries and gives birth to the sons and daughters of men."[3]

This is not simply a biological fact, the Holy Father added, but an insight into the distinctive character and role of women in the world. Think about the Catholic women (and families) who adopt children, godparent children, and catechize children in the myriad programs in Catholic parishes. Their maternal leadership brings children up in the Mystical Body of Christ, the Church. What women's stories do you know about adoptive families, catechetical leaders, or godparents who made a significant difference in children's lives? Are you such a woman?

Walking in the New Evangelization
by Kelly Wahlquist

As we conclude this chapter, think about what new insights or "God prompts" you have experienced as you reflected on the experiences of these women. Here are a couple of ways you can continue to reflect upon what you have discovered in the coming week!

Contemplate Your Own Gifts

Easter Sunday is traditionally a day to wear new clothes, to note the change of season, and hopefully, to celebrate good weather. Write a prayer letter to the risen Jesus asking him for an inner newness in your heart. What gifts do you need for a renewed prayer life? What gifts do you need for a renewed sense of peace? What gifts do you need to increase your faith in God, hope in your own holiness, and love of the Mystical Body of Christ, the Church? Along with your gratitude for a new beginning, write your petitions to the Lord. Tuck your letter in your bible, or perhaps in this book, and be sure to read it on Easter.

Faith in Action

Many Christians and non-Christians only attend church on Easter Sunday. Something in the human psyche wants to celebrate life! Think about some of your family Easter traditions; how do they speak to you about life? Reflect back on what Easter was like as a child. Plan an Easter celebration for your family and friends, at which you will celebrate the life of the risen Christ as never before. Make a guest list, and follow through!

6.

The Gift of the Holy Spirit
(Pentecost)

A Moment to Ponder
by Kelly Wahlquist

Of all the gifts God has bestowed upon us, the gift of the Holy Spirit surpasses them all as the source of every gift. We pray to the Spirit as the Lord, the giver of life. The Spirit gives us the divine life. In Baptism, God has given us a share in his divine life.

Just sit with that for a moment: the God of the universe dwells within us.

The Holy Spirit equips us to grow in holiness and to live as disciples of Christ. The Holy Spirit empowers us to be bold in living and proclaiming the faith with confidence, conviction, and hope. The Holy Spirit "opens us to understand better the things of God, human things, situations, all things."[1]

Mary's relationship with the Holy Spirit inspires our own! Just as Mary's *fiat*, her yes to God, opened her to greater things, so too is it with us. That's why the Spirit glories in our receptivity! Our yes cooperates with the Spirit's genius!

Receptivity to the Spirit edifies all the gifts! The Spirit's abundance multiplies and expands our generosity, enabling self-donating love. Sensitivity, touched by the Spirit's inspiration, becomes a holy listening to the hearts of others and moves us to care for them. When we yield our gift of maternity to the Spirit, the Spirit increases the fruitful yield of those we birth and nurture for God's kingdom. And finally, the Spirit's inward promptings urge us to pray and ponder faithfully, so we may always know God's will.

You have been given an incredible gift in the Holy Spirit. If you haven't completely opened it yet, you're going to want to start tearing away the wrappings because unwrapping this gift will perfect all your gifts and allow you to nurture the Body of Christ, to build up his kingdom on earth, and to live your life giving glory to God!

> Come, Holy Spirit! Fill the hearts of thy faithful ones,
> and enkindle in them the fire of thy love.
> Grant, O merciful Father,
> that thy Divine Spirit may enlighten, inflame and purify us,
> that he may penetrate us with his heavenly dew
> and make us fruitful in good works,
> through Our Lord Jesus Christ, thy Son, who with thee,
> in the unity of the same Spirit, lives and reigns, one God,
> forever and ever. Amen. (from the *Litany of the Holy Spirit*)

Enter the Scripture
by Sarah Christmyer

In this final week we will delve into the lectionary readings most commonly associated with the descent of the Holy Spirit at Pentecost: John 7:37–39 (Vigil Mass), and John 20:19–23 (Sunday Mass), as well as the optional readings John 15:26–27, 16:12–15 (B), and John 14:15–16, 23b–26 (C).

Passover was just one of three great pilgrim feasts, and the second came just seven weeks later. The feast of Pentecost (or Shavuot, also known as the "Feast of Weeks") was a grand celebration of thanks for God's bounty. Families from all over the land joined their neighbors and streamed toward Jerusalem bearing the first fruits of the harvest: barley, wheat, olives, dates, pomegranates, and figs piled in baskets and decorated with grapes. Two loaves of bread from the new wheat crop were brought for dedication at the Temple. Young and old, rich and poor, came together by district and made their offerings accompanied by music and the blare of trumpets. It was a joyous time.

The feast eventually became associated with God's giving of the Torah on Mount Sinai, fifty days after the first Passover and release from Egypt. It was the day Israel entered a covenant with God, and it was celebrated as a renewal of that covenant.

Passover and Pentecost were linked by a ritual called the "Counting of the Omer."[2] Starting on the second day of Passover, in every home, after every sundown, a blessing was said, and the week and day was named until seven weeks of seven days were counted out. Imagine a giant Advent calendar ticking off forty-nine days, with everyone you know joining in the count. Anticipation was tangible. It built until it climaxed at the feast.

In the midst of this, the disciples of Jesus anticipated something else. Death had not held Jesus back. For forty days after his resurrection, he appeared to many witnesses. They wondered whether he would restore the kingdom to Israel, which he had announced during his ministry. But he told them instead of the coming of "the counselor," "the spirit of truth." This "holy spirit, whom the father will send," would continue to teach them and enable them to bear witness to the truth even through persecution.[3] In spite of their fear of the authorities, Jesus charged his disciples to stay in Jerusalem. For "before many days you shall be baptized with the Holy

Spirit . . . and you shall receive power . . . and you shall be my witnesses in Jerusalem and in all Judea and Samar'ia and to the end of the earth" (Acts 1:5, 8).

Whether they understood what was meant by this, we don't know. But the disciples didn't throw themselves into preparations for Shavuot; rather, they returned to the Upper Room and "devoted themselves to prayer" (Acts 1:14). Mary was with them: Mary, who was overshadowed by the Holy Spirit at the Annunciation and who received the word from God that Jesus is the expected Messiah; whose life of prayerful pondering and mothering of Jesus prepared her to mother the whole Body of Christ—starting with John, and now in this Upper Room. Surely she prayed for the gift of the Spirit, for herself and for them. Surely she held them in her heart, preparing them to receive the Spirit and be born as the Church—just as she held Jesus in her womb until the time was ripe.

There is no way to know whether the disciples kept counting off the weeks and days of the Omer as they prayed, or if they were thinking of the Lord giving the Torah at Mount Sinai when Pentecost arrived. I have to think that they did. Passover kicked off a time of waiting for Pentecost. The omer of barley that was offered then anticipated the first fruits to be offered in seven weeks. Likewise, Israel's liberation from Egypt anticipated what would happen at Sinai. It started them on a journey to where they would enter a covenant with God, become his people, and receive the Torah to guide their ways. That pair of events—Passover and Pentecost, with the forty-nine-day journey between—enabled Israel to become the kingdom of God.

Jesus had transformed the Passover at the Last Supper, illuminating it and filling it with new meaning. He had announced the coming of the kingdom. Would he not change Pentecost too?

"When the time for Pentecost was fulfilled" (Acts 2:1, NAB), the disciples gathered in the Upper Room on Mount Zion. Suddenly, the sound of a mighty wind filled the house.

Tongues of fire rested on each of them, filling them with the Holy Spirit; this event was reminiscent of the noise and fire that marked the descent of the Lord on Mount Sinai. Back then, all the people "took their stand at the foot of the mountain" when the Lord descended in fire and thunder (Ex 19:17). Now the multitude of people gathered in Jerusalem for Pentecost were coming together at the sound of the Spirit's descent on Mount Zion (see Acts 2:6). The people at Mount Sinai were afraid and asked Moses to hear God on their behalf. But the people at Mount Zion heard the disciples proclaiming the works of God in their own languages. They may have gathered in Jerusalem to renew the old covenant made with Moses, but now the Holy Spirit was offering the promise of the new covenant in Jesus Christ.

Many years before, Jeremiah prophesied, "Behold, the days are coming, says the LORD, when I will make a new covenant with the house of Israel . . . not like the covenant which I made with their fathers when I took them by the hand to bring them out of the land of Egypt. . . . *I will put my law within them, and I will write it upon their hearts; and I will be their God, and they shall be my people*" (Jer 31:31–33, emphasis mine).

Once he brought them out of Egypt and gave them his written law. Now that he has brought them out of bondage from sin and death, he will write his new law on their hearts by the power of the Holy Spirit. Those baptized by the Spirit will be his new people of the new covenant. This is the start of his kingdom, the Church. And "three thousand souls" were baptized that day (Acts 2:41)—the first fruits of a tremendous "harvest" of Christians that had only begun (see Jn 4:35)!

Walk in Her Sandals: Anah's Story

by Stephanie Landsem

He had risen! Jesus had risen from the dead.

Anah piled the last of the rounds of bread in a basket and hefted it on top of her head. Even now, weeks later, the thought filled her with a rush of amazement. Jesus had worked miracles among them, but this was different. This changed everything; their world, their history, and their very nature and being had been transformed on that morning that he'd appeared to her mother and Mary Magdalene.

That morning, after the Sabbath, when her mother had burst into the courtyard with Mary Magdalene, the two women had glowed—glowed!—with a brilliance that seemed to come from within. Their words tripped over each other: a light, the tomb, an angel, and finally, Jesus himself.

The men didn't believe it—at least, not at first.

James thought his mother had gone mad, that grief had broken her. "You're talking nonsense." But Miriam and Mary Magdalene had just laughed—a joy-filled laugh that seemed to fill the courtyard with sunshine.

That morning weeks ago, Anah had helped Miriam and Mary Magdalene search Jerusalem for Peter. They found him at the house of Nicodemus. When he heard the women's story, Peter shouted, "The body was gone?"

"Yes, the angel—"

"The guards were there?"

"Yes, but they were—"

"Someone stole his body! They stole our Lord's body." He jumped and ran out of the house, followed by John. By the time Anah had arrived breathless at the tomb, Peter and John had already found it empty.

They questioned Miriam relentlessly, but she said the same thing over and over. "Do not be afraid. He is risen!"

Do not be afraid. The words had stayed with her, like a lingering song. Do not be afraid to believe in him. Do not be afraid to follow him. In the weeks that followed, Jesus had appeared to the disciples, spoken to them, and even eaten with them. She listened to the stories, and her faith had grown like a seed finally given water and sunlight. Even the sorrow over her barren womb had been soothed by this new faith and hope.

Anah pushed through the courtyard gate, steadying the basket on her head and quickening her steps to catch up with Miriam. "Why such a hurry today?"

"Peter. He said to come quickly." Miriam answered in a breathless voice.

Miriam and Huldah cared for the disciples and the ever-increasing group of believers like their own children, bringing them bread, wine, and comfort. And since the day Jesus had left the tomb, Zilpah spent her days in prayer, her body growing frailer but her will stronger than ever. Even Veronica had found new purpose. Joses listened to what the scribes heard from the Pharisees, and Veronica carried his messages and warnings to the disciples.

There was much to do, and Anah did it willingly, yet she still felt unfulfilled. What was her place in this new life? Her purpose? Was she unworthy to have her own part in the communion of believers, just as she had been unworthy to be mother to a child?

As Miriam and Anah neared the Temple, the crowd thickened. She'd never seen so many pilgrims in Jerusalem for Pentecost. Were they here because they'd heard of Jesus? A line of blue-garbed men eyed the crowd with sharp eyes: Temple guards. Anah knew who they were looking for, Peter and the others.

Miriam glanced back, a warning in her eyes.

Anah pulled her head covering over her face. If just one guard recognized them and knew their connection with Jesus, they would be followed.

She lowered her eyes and caught up with her mother as she crossed the bridge into the center of the city. For weeks, Anah had wondered at the disciples. Would Jesus, who had no fear of the Pharisees, have wanted his followers to hide in fear? Peter had shown himself to be a coward the night Jesus had been taken. He and the others had doubted Miriam and Mary Magdalene on the morning of the empty tomb. Thomas had even doubted when his own brothers had seen Jesus in the upper room that first time. Is that really what these men were? Cowards and doubters? How long would they hide?

Then, more than a week ago, James had burst into the courtyard, his face alight with joy. They had seen Jesus, and he had brought them to Mount Olivet, just outside Jerusalem.

"He told us—all of us—everything written about him must be fulfilled. Then—I don't know how—but it seemed . . . I understood, completely understood the Law, the prophets, and psalms. As if my mind had been closed and now it is opened."

Joses and the women gathered around him. "And what now? Did he tell you what to do now?" Joses asked the question on Anah's lips.

James took a deep breath. "He said, 'I'm sending the promise of my Father upon you,' but to stay in the city until we are clothed with power from on high."

"Power?" Joses raised his brows. "What kind of power? Power to defeat the Sanhedrin?"

"I don't know. Perhaps. Perhaps strength, or weapons and the men to use them."

Swords and soldiers? Everything Anah had heard about Jesus told her that would not be the power he would send. But she kept her thoughts to herself.

Anah knelt in front of her brother. "What does Peter say?"

James rubbed a hand over his eyes and down his beard. "The same as he's said for weeks: wait and pray."

Wait and pray. They had been waiting and praying for almost ten days now. *How much longer, Lord?*

Anah and Miriam turned down a side street and slowed. Anah checked for the blue robe of a Temple guard or the wide tassels of a Pharisee spy. There were only women clustered at the corner with their water jars. Miriam nodded. She opened a courtyard gate, and they slipped inside.

They climbed the steep outdoor stairs to the flat roof and pushed open the door to a room filled with men, women, and even some Gentiles. Heavy fabric covered the windows to keep out prying eyes, making the room shadowy and dim. Anah followed Miriam to join Mary, Mary Magdalene, and some of the other women along the wall.

The disciples stood near the front, arguing. "Let us go out, as he said, and proclaim him to all the nations. See," Thomas motioned to the men and women crowding into the upper room, "already, we have more than a hundred believers."

"A hundred men and women who will be arrested and put in prison if the Sanhedrin knows about them," answered Peter. "He told us to wait. We will wait."

Anah eyed the crowd as the men debated and the women whispered. With all these people, it wouldn't be long before the Pharisees found them anyway. Would the power James spoke of save them all from the Temple guards?

Anah heard a strange noise amid the chatter. What was it? A low hum, like a soft wind rustling through the trees or the chime of distant bells. The women stopped talking.

"Can you hear it?" Huldah whispered.

Miriam's brow furrowed as she looked to the door. But the sound wasn't coming from outside.

The men fell silent.

The sound became like a waterfall, rushing over rocks. The women drew closer together. From the front of the room, Peter began to pray in the words Jesus had taught them.

"Our Father, who art in heaven . . ."

The murmur of a steady wind filled the room, although not a fringe or tassel swayed. Anah's heart sped up. What was happening? Miriam took Anah's hand, her grip firm and reassuring.

". . . hallowed be Thy name."

A flickering glow lit the dimness. The glow separated and dispersed, resting above each person, suffusing each in light like a candle in the darkness. Anah put a hand to her face. Was she too glowing?

"Thy kingdom come . . ."

The sound rose to a roar, as if a storm had broken upon them, yet not one man or woman moved. A sudden warmth rushed from the top of Anah's head to her feet. At the same time, a great chasm seemed to open inside her. The chasm deepened and began to be filled—with the breath of wind at the dawn, with sunlight, and with warmth like the rays of the setting sun. She saw nothing but bright light, heard nothing but the wind, and felt nothing but her own heartbeat and pure joy.

"Lead us not into temptation, but deliver us from evil."

She could see again. Her mother's eyes were wide, and tears glimmered on her face. Huldah stood open mouthed. The glow of the light melted away—sinking into each person's skin—and then, silence.

She touched her face. She was filled, like a jar, overflowing with the finest wine, but lighter than wine, like sunlight and dew. And in the center of her being, a fire, burning with a fervor she'd never known. He had filled her—he had filled her emptiness—with this power from on high. But what was she to do with it?

She gazed at the men and women in the room—those who had followed Jesus for years and those who had never met him but still believed; from the look on their faces, they too burned with the fire.

Peter stood very tall in the middle of the room. "Now," he said. "Now is the time. Let us go to the Temple."

As if one body, they rushed outside. The men clattered down the stairs. The women moved as if floating on air. Anah felt lighter than the motes of dust in the sunlight yet as full as a jar brimming with the choicest wine. She had prayed for a child—to perhaps still be a mother if God willed it—to fill her emptiness. But now, the emptiness was gone. The need for purpose and meaning in her life was satisfied in a way she could never have foreseen.

People turned to stare as the believers—like a flock guided by an invisible shepherd—streamed through the Temple gates and into the court of the Gentiles. John and Peter wore the focused bearing of soldiers. James leapt into the air with a shout. Some of the others—Andrew, Matthew, and Thomas—cried out, "Alleluia!"

"Are they drunk?" A woman holding her offering of grain asked a matron beside her.

"They've had too much of the new wine." Her friend answered with a laugh.

An older scribe scowled. "The priests will deal with this." He hurried toward the portico where the priests convened. Anah couldn't help but smile. Had it been just minutes—or hours—ago when she had feared the priests and the Temple guards? She had no room for fear in her now. And neither did the disciples.

Peter and John marched up the steps to stand in front of the Beautiful Gate. Peter began to speak, his voice loud and sure. "People, listen to me."

The pilgrims—from lands throughout the empire—gathered around. Could they see the fire of the spirit in Peter's eyes, the light emanating from John's face? How could they not?

Peter raised his hands over them. "You who are Jews, indeed all of you staying in Jerusalem, listen to me. These men are not drunk, as you suppose. No," his voice grew even stronger, "this was spoken through the prophet Joel: 'It will come to pass in the last days that I will pour out a portion of my spirit upon all flesh. Your sons and your daughters shall prophesy, your young men shall see visions, and your old men shall dream dreams.' This is the time! Listen to what we say, and that same spirit will be poured upon you."

Peter nodded to James, John, and Andrew. The men fanned out, each approaching a group of pilgrims as if directed by an invisible hand.

Andrew approached the group of Cyrenians, and as he opened his mouth, words she couldn't understand came out. Next to her, a man spoke to his dark-skinned neighbor. "Is that man not one of the Galileans? How does he know the language of my homeland?"

"And that one," the dark man said, pointing to John, "he is speaking in my tongue, the language of Egypt."

Now all the disciples went through the crowd, speaking loudly and with great excitement in languages Anah had never heard, shouts of amazement following in their wake.

"It is the work of the Lord," said a man with pale skin and hair the color of ripe wheat. "I hear him speak the words of my homeland in the north."

A group of priests pushed past her, the scribe she'd seen earlier leading the way. "These are the men you seek." He pointed to Peter, who took no notice of them.

One of the priests, a Pharisee with wide phylacteries and narrowed eyes, surveyed the excited pilgrims. "If we try to arrest them now, the crowd will turn against us."

But Anah knew it wasn't the crowd, as the priest claimed. The power of the Spirit protected them all, just as Jesus had foretold. These men, the disciples of Jesus whom she had secretly deemed cowards, were now courageous prophets. These doubters were now deliverers of the Spirit that possessed them. Just minutes earlier, they had been afraid, but now they would spend the rest of their lives telling anyone who would listen about Jesus.

"What do we do?" a young well-dressed man shouted to Peter.

"Repent and be baptized!"

The mass of people surged toward Peter and the Beautiful Gate.

The fire quickened in her own heart, as if urging her on. Who was she to tell? What was her purpose now? She closed her eyes. *Spirit of truth, guide me. To whom shall I go? To whom shall I speak your name?*

She opened her eyes. Near the portico a group of women huddled together, pointing at the disciples, staying in the shadows. One, a matron with doubting eyes and pinched mouth, frowned. A girl with shining auburn hair watched with skeptical eyes. Beside her, a young mother with a child in her arms leaned forward, as if wishing to step forward but unsure. Anah started toward the women, swimming against the flood of pilgrims.

A sense of rightness, of certainty, suffused her.

Just weeks ago, Jesus had ridden into Jerusalem like a king, but Anah had doubted. Women she loved—her mother, Huldah, and Mary Magdalene—had opened her heart to Jesus. Now, she would do the same, for old women and young, for the childless and those with children in their arms, and for those who were seeking and those who needed to be found.

Yes. This is my purpose.

She approached the women and smiled at the young mother. "Peace be with you," she said to them. "My sisters, I am Anah. I can tell you about Jesus. Oh, how my heart is burning to tell you!"

Unwrap the Gift of the Holy Spirit
by Pat Gohn

Scripture tells us that God is spirit (see Jn 4:24)—that the one who created the whole world is neither male nor female—despite the fact that Christ was a man and referred to God as his Father (see Jn 5:17–18). And yet, the catechism tells us that "God's parental tenderness can also be expressed by the image of motherhood" (CCC, 239). Specifically, it is the Holy Spirit whose presence comforts, nurtures, and guides us, whether hovering over the waters at Creation, in the great cloud of glory that led the Chosen People through the wilderness, or resting upon the apostles in the Upper Room, causing them to break forth in animated joy. And so, as we open ourselves to the Holy Spirit, we are embracing all that is good and unique about our calling, our vocation, and ourselves.

The Holy Spirit is the glory of God in action—our ultimate teacher and guide. Our call as Christians is to be docile to the

Spirit's leading, to be moldable, teachable, and coachable. This is especially true in the years following the sacrament of Confirmation. To be confirmed in the Spirit means we are willing to be led and willing to be sent. (If Confirmation is a distant memory for you, consider going to confession and asking a priest to pray with you for a fresh outpouring of grace.)

In God's great economy there is room for all the gifts of women, room to serve and room to grow. When the Holy Spirit animates our life, our gifts will grow toward perfection. Even today we can pray that the Holy Spirit sets us on fire for the glory of God!

As we look at the gift of the Holy Spirit in light of Pentecost, we cannot help but look to Mary, whom the Church calls "the spouse" of the Holy Spirit. She was intimately acquainted with the Spirit long before the others. Mary's relationship with the Holy Spirit began in the womb, where God fashioned her without stain of sin, in preparation for the invitation he would send when she was older. Conceived without sin, she willingly surrendered her own plans to the will of God. More to the point, Mary united her will with the will of God out of love. With her full consent at the Annunciation, the Holy Spirit overshadowed her and she conceived the Christ.

The Holy Spirit continued working through Mary all through her life and ordered her life toward holiness and loving service to God. Mary is a role model for the life of the Spirit.

Mary models fidelity to Christ and his Church. She is called the first disciple of Jesus. She was there when Jesus' life on earth began and when it ended. In Bethlehem she lovingly introduced Jesus to all those who came in homage before him (see Mt 2:9–11). While there are many hidden years in the life of Jesus that only Mary knows about, she was present to him as Mother and teacher. At the end of Christ's life, the Spirit strengthened and equipped Mary at the cross (see Jn 19:30). She not only endured her intense pain and sorrow at the crucifixion but also accepted Jesus' final request (see Jn

19:26–27) to become a spiritual Mother to all the disciples. Mary's fidelity to the Church continued through Pentecost's birth of the nascent Church.

Mary lived her vocation well and performed pious actions. She raised her Son alongside her husband, in their Jewish faith, and in the daily life beyond the Temple. She followed the Law of Moses (Lk 2:39–40).

Mary's life was one of generous service. We see her rendering loving care toward the older Elizabeth at the Visitation (see Lk 1:39–50) and sensitivity toward the bride and groom at the wedding at Cana (see Jn 2:1–12). In the course of Jesus' public ministry, she was a witness to others of doing the will of God and tending to the needs of the community, right up through Pentecost.

Mary had a prayer life. Scripture offers evidence of her many ponderings (see Lk 2:19, 51) on the mysteries of God. These references show us that Mary's interior life was a priority.

Mary knew the joy of the Gospel. She said,

> My soul magnifies the Lord,
> and my spirit rejoices in God my Savior,
> for he has regarded the low estate of his handmaiden.
> For behold, henceforth all generations will call me
> blessed;
> for he who is mighty has done great things for me,
> and holy is his name. (Lk 1:46–49)

How is the Holy Spirit calling you to imitate the Spirit-led life of the Blessed Mother today?

As you come to Pentecost, consider the gift of the Holy Spirit:

1. Think about how you have experienced the presence of the Holy Spirit in your life. How would you describe this encounter?

2. Mary continued to surrender to the Holy Spirit throughout her life as described here. Which do you think was easiest—or most difficult?

3. What is one way you would like to grow in your relationship with the Holy Spirit?

Reflect on the Meaning: Pentecost
by Barbara Heil

I made it to the airport just in time and checked my two bags at the counter as I breathed a sigh of relief. I did it! With everything going on, and everything that had happened that morning, I had still made it.

I headed toward passenger screening, thinking of which coffee place to head to on my way to my flight. Suddenly I stopped in my tracks. I had never seen the security line at the airport, *my* airport, so long! What were all these people doing here? The sun wasn't even up yet!

The line snaked around, sometimes two or three people wide, and had spilled out from the security area. I frowned and looked at my watch. This better go quickly or I'll miss my coffee! After twenty minutes I was still standing there. Forget coffee! This better go quickly or I'll miss my flight! The line hardly seemed to move as the time on my watch flew by. Now I really was in danger of missing my flight.

I was scheduled to speak that night, so I didn't have a lot of other options to get there on time. Should I go back to the counter? Should I stay in line and keep going forward? My frustration was growing, as well as everyone else's. Airport security was still new, still confusing, and we were told not to use our cell phones. I've got to go; I've got to do something! I can't just stand here anymore!

To my left, I noticed people were just breezing through a line. It was the line for passengers in a higher level of a mileage rewards program. *I had that program.* I looked at my boarding pass and then quietly, almost sheepishly, slipped under the rope separating the lines. I had been just standing there even though I was holding the right to be in the faster line the whole time. I breezed through security and onto my flight that was ready to finish boarding.

I was laughing, half embarrassed at myself, glad no one I knew had witnessed my morning. In my seat on the plane I started to think about it. All that time I was inwardly grumbling, nervous, and anxious, to the point of becoming resentful—you name it—while at the same time I was unknowingly holding the right, the privilege, and a status that changed everything. Wow.

How often are we like that? We try to get by on our own, in our own power. We give in to the temptation to think that everything is up to us. We become frustrated, worrying that we are going to miss something, and living with a vague sense of desire, without knowing what we are hungering for. And all the while, we are holding on to something that changes everything!

When Pentecost comes, we see the Holy Spirit, *God's own Spirit*, descending from the Father. He didn't just fill the disciples; he filled all those gathered in the upper chamber, including Mary! And he didn't stop there. In the book of the Acts of the Apostles, we see that every time people believed in Jesus and received what the apostles taught, the Holy Spirit descended in the same way that he did on the Church's first Pentecost. He filled the new believers with the Holy Spirit. And it changed them.

Jesus told his disciples, "It is to your advantage that I go away, for if I don't go away, the Counselor [*Parakletos*, comforter, helper, counselor, advocate; literally, one who comes alongside!] will not come to you; but if I go, I will send him to you" (Jn 16:7, 16). Imagine that. Jesus said it was actually good that he was leaving, so that the Holy Spirit could come. We would not be orphans.

At Pentecost, be reminded of the Holy Spirit that you received at Baptism, and the fullness of the Holy Spirit that you received at Confirmation. You didn't just receive a rite of passage; you received the same Holy Spirit that was poured out on Pentecost! *This is the same Holy Spirit that raised Christ from the dead!* The same Holy Spirit that filled and empowered the early Church to live and declare the Gospel that changed the world! Some may profess a love for Christ but don't know much about what happened on Pentecost, and who the Holy Spirit even is. Some are even afraid. Even his name, Holy Spirit, can seem so mysterious.

It is the Holy Spirit that gives us the power to live as disciples of Jesus, to grow in holiness, filled with sacrificial love. It is the Holy Spirit that gives us understanding, awakens us, emboldens us, and fills us to overflowing. We are not alone! He is the one we hunger for, and he is stirring us to go deeper, to open ourselves to him in a new way, allowing him to overflow in our lives, renew our hearts and minds, and change us into Christ's own image. He isn't calling us to the impossible mission of doing this ourselves, of changing ourselves by ourselves. It is the Holy Spirit that is at work, in us and in his Church, causing us to live as sons and daughters of God.

Invite him to have his way in your life. Ask him to teach you how to open to him and how to cooperate with his movement and action. The Father sent him, and we need him! Let us be filled again with the outpouring of Pentecost, to receive more fully, so we can pour him out. Welcome, Holy Spirit!

Lectio for Pentecost

Read Acts 2:1–4, and read it a second time more slowly. Then read it for a third time, noting the words or thoughts that jump out at you.

> When the day of Pentecost had come, they were all together in one place. And suddenly a sound came from heaven like the rush of a mighty wind, and it filled all

the house where they were sitting. And there appeared to them tongues as of fire, distributed and resting on each one of them. And they were all filled with the Holy Spirit and began to speak in other tongues, as the Spirit gave them utterance.

Now, ask yourself:

- What do I hear? (Write down the words or phrases that stand out to you as you read.)

- What does it mean? (Write down what you think about those words, or why you think they're important.)

- What is Jesus saying to me? (Write what you hear Jesus saying into your heart, and respond to him.)

Questions for Group Discussion
by Dr. Carol Younger

1. *Enter the Scripture.* Pentecost is the birthday of the Church, yet you'd be hard-pressed to find a Pentecost countdown calendar filled with chocolate. People don't prepare for this "birth" as they do for the birth of Christ, but the Church does—and so should we. What are some practical ways we can prepare for Pentecost as we journey through the fifty days from the Resurrection of the Lord to the coming of the Holy Spirit? How have you celebrated Pentecost with your family or in your church? How can we live the spirit of Pentecost throughout the year?

2. *Walk in Her Sandals.* Anah is carrying bread at the beginning of her story, taking it to the disciples who wait for the promised Spirit. In one of those in-between times of the spiritual life, Anah continues her constant care for others. What are those constants of your spiritual life that carry you through the "waiting" times? What works of mercy do you choose to perform? Anah's inner fear and her lack

of purpose still bother her, even after Jesus' resurrection. At Pentecost, the Spirit transforms the world's notion of power and purpose. His confirming grace settles doubts, converts hearts. Anah begins to share her blessings in Jesus. Recall a time when you spoke to another of the truth of your Catholic faith, unafraid and with personal conviction. Share what happened.

3. *Unwrap the Gift*. The Holy Spirit dwells in those who surrender to him. Mary lived fidelity, generosity, and joy because of her surrender to the Holy Spirit. Her life is one of magnifying the Lord, rejoicing in the Spirit within her. On your spiritual journey, when has the Spirit come and asked for your surrender to his will? It might have happened in prayer. Or it might have occurred in an event, or in a relationship with another. When did you know it was the Spirit? What did you say to his invitation to surrender?

4. *Reflect on the Meaning*. Pentecost Mass includes a special reading of the Pentecost Sequence of the Holy Spirit: *Veni, Sancte Spiritus*. In an exclamatory tone, we hear, "Come, Holy Spirit, come! And from your celestial home shed a ray of light divine! Come, Father of the poor! Come, source of all our store! Come, within our bosoms shine." The prayer goes on and ends with, "On the faithful, who adore, and confess you, evermore. In your sevenfold gift descend: Give them virtue's sure reward; Give them your salvation, Lord; Give them joys that never end."

   Dig deep in memories, and relive a joyous day at your parish, at a wedding, a Confirmation, or a Baptism, a day when you smiled the whole day because you were so happy just to be there! What did the Holy Spirit do to infuse such intense joy into the occasion? As you recall that day, for what do you want to thank the Holy Spirit?

Walking in the New Evangelization
by *Kelly Wahlquist*

As we conclude this final chapter of the book, think about what new insights or "God prompts" you have experienced. Here are a couple of ways you can continue to reflect upon what you have discovered!

Contemplate Your Own Gifts

Perhaps the idea that you can have your own relationship with the Holy Spirit is new or novel to you. Don't be afraid! Find a quiet place, close your eyes, and simply invite the Holy Spirit to occupy your heart. If you wish, you can use this traditional prayer attributed to Cardinal Mercier: "Holy Spirit, Soul of my soul, I adore you. Enlighten, guide, strengthen, and console me. Tell me what I ought to do and command me to do it. I promise to be submissive in everything that you permit to happen to me, only show me what is your will."

Then meditate on and write down brief answers to the following: Where do I need enlightenment? In what aspects of my life do I need guidance right now? What strengths do I need increased? What consolations do I ask of the Holy Spirit? Keep this small paper, bringing it out once a month to pray over.

Faith in Action

Ask the Holy Spirit to reveal your gifts to you. Ask him to give you the courage to use the gifts and the wisdom to discern where to use your gifts. Ask him to reveal how God has equipped you to bring others to the risen Lord.

Perhaps you are being called to

- make an appointment and introduce yourself to the leader of the RCIA program in your parish;

- ask about the program of sponsorship for Confirmation candidates, and consider and pray about becoming a sponsor; or

- volunteer to be part of the prayer support team.

Listen to what the Holy Spirit is saying, and actively build God's kingdom on earth!

Conclusion

by Kelly Wahlquist

> God, infinitely perfect and blessed in himself, in a plan
> of sheer goodness freely created man to make him share
> in his own blessed life. For this reason, at every time and
> in every place, God draws close to man. He calls man to
> seek him, to know him, to love him with all his strength.
> —*Catechism of the Catholic Church*, 1

At every time and in every place, God is drawing us closer
to him. He thirsts that we might thirst for him (*CCC*, 2561).
Yet, how many times do we miss those moments, or perhaps
not grasp the depth of the greatness they offer? How often do
we miss the encounter because we are caught in the monot-
ony? What if we embraced each repetitive encounter with the
heart of one who thirsts? What if we embraced each repetitive
moment with the heart of a child (see Mt 18:3)?

I like what G. K. Chesterton says about repetition:

> Because children have abounding vitality, because they
> are in spirit fierce and free, therefore, they want things
> repeated and unchanged. They always say, "Do it again";
> and the grown-up person does it again until he is nearly
> dead. For grown-up people are not strong enough to
> exult in monotony. But perhaps God is strong enough
> to exult in monotony. It is possible that God says every
> morning, "Do it again" to the sun; and every evening,
> "Do it again" to the moon. It may not be automatic
> necessity that makes all daisies alike; it may be that God
> makes every daisy separately, but has never got tired of
> making them. It may be that He has the eternal appetite
> of infancy; for we have sinned and grown old, and our
> Father is younger than we.[1]

139

In all of life there is beauty found in repetition, from breathing in and out to the rising and setting of the sun, and in our everyday activities. If we allow ourselves to have an eternal appetite, to exult in each repetition, we open ourselves up to a powerful and transformative encounter with God. God, who uses every opportunity to draw us back to him, reaches out to us and teaches us through repetition. As children who concentrate on their every wobbly step while learning to master the skill of walking, attentiveness to the actions we repeat can help us perfect our walk on this journey back to the heart of the Father.

We see the power of repetition in our prayers. The Rosary is a beautiful example of praying in repetition such that we enter into a meditation on the life of Christ. We see the power of repetition in the greatest of all prayers, the Mass. And we experience the life-changing power of repetition in our liturgical year. When repetition is not done aimlessly but rather entered into with an excited-to-learn "do it again" heart of a child, the result is a more perfect union with God. And each year, the Church, in its wisdom, allows us to prepare our hearts and welcome Jesus in a new and deeper way, to walk with him in his passion, and to become more like him as we join the mission to build up his kingdom.

Knowing that God can and does use repetition, I shouldn't be surprised that the message the Holy Spirit put on my heart on a crisp autumn morning to heal the Body of Christ—the message that was fueled in prayer on Good Friday to create a way for women to enter more fully into Christ's passion—had come full circle a year later as I once again prayed after Communion with the sun shining through the leafless trees into the chapel at Pacem in Terris Retreat Center.

As I meditated on the Gospel in the beautiful serene retreat setting, it hit me: when we enter into something with the openness and hunger of a child, God not only feeds us abundantly; he provides us with extra nourishment along the way. I can't help but think that every time I am at Pacem in

Terris. I not only leave peaceful, but I take a piece of Pacem back with me. Even though I have been there countless times before, I always encounter God anew, because it is a repetitive action that I enter into with a "do-it-again" attitude.

As you enter into the many "Lents" of your life, it is our hope that *Walk in Her Sandals* has inspired you to do so with a new and fresh eternal appetite. We pray that in the pages of this book you experienced a renewal in your spirit to enter into the passion, death, resurrection, and mission of Jesus with the heart of the woman you were created to be and the "do-it-again" outlook of the child of God that you are. May you take a piece of this book with you in all that you do, be that the riches of the scriptures that were illuminated, the beauty of knowing your giftedness as a woman, or the lessons found in the fictional stories of the women who walked with Jesus. Above all, may you come to know of the glory of God as you walk in *your* sandals alongside our Lord.

Notes

Introduction

1. Pontifical Council for Justice and Peace, "Compendium of the Catholic Social Doctrine of the Church," 2005, http://www.vatican.va.

1. The Gift of Receptivity (Palm Sunday)

1. The gospels call the animal variously a colt (the foal of a donkey) and a donkey (or ass), and Matthew says Jesus requested both. Each gospel writer in his own way shows how the Lord's request reflects the prophecy of Zechariah 9:9.

2. *Messiah* and *Christ* both mean "anointed one"; they refer to Israel's expected king.

2. The Gift of Generosity (Holy Thursday)

1. This timing is consistent in the synoptic gospels. In contrast, John suggests that the Passover began several hours after Jesus' death. For a discussion of solutions proposed to this seeming discrepancy, see "When Did Jesus Celebrate the Last Supper?" in *Ignatius Catholic Study Bible* (San Francisco: Ignatius Press, 2010), 188.

2. See John 10:17–18 to see how John echoes these words of Jesus in his description of Jesus' laying aside and taking up his garments at the Last Supper.

3. Psalms 113–118, six "hallel" or praise psalms, were recited at the three pilgrim festivals and on other holy days. At the Seder meal, Psalm 113 (and sometimes 114) was sung before dinner, and the rest were sung after the grace after meals. This "Lesser Hallel" was capped off by the Great Hallel, Psalm 136.

3. The Gift of Sensitivity (Good Friday)

1. Cicero, *Against Verres* 2.5.165.

2. Josephus, *Jewish War* 7.203.

3. John Paul II, *Letter to Women*, June 29, 1995, http://w2.vatican.va.

4. Dwight Longnecker, "The Biology of the Annunciation," *National Catholic Register*, March 20, 2006, http://www.ncregister.com.

5. Jeff Cavins, *When You Suffer: Biblical Keys for Hope and Understanding* (Cincinnati: Franciscan Media, 2015), 1.

4. The Gift of Prayer (Holy Saturday)

1. Responsory, Divine Office for Holy Saturday.

5. The Gift of Maternity (Easter Sunday)

1. Benedict XVI, "General Audience," February 14, 2007, quoting *Super Ioannem*, ed. Cai, 2519, http://w2.vatican.va.

2. John Paul II, *Mulieris Dignitatem*, August 15, 1988, no. 30.

3. "The Church Must Address the Role of Women," *Vatican Information Service*, October 14, 2013, http://visnews-en.blogspot.com.

6. The Gift of the Holy Spirit (Pentecost)

1. Francis, General Audience, April 30, 2014.

2. An omer of barley was cut and offered to God on the second day of the week-long Passover festival, and from that day on, seven weeks of seven days were counted out (see Lv 23:16). The day after the forty-ninth—the fiftieth—was Shavuot/Pentecost.

3. See Jn 14:15–16, 23b–26; 15:26–27; 16:12–15.

Conclusion

1. G. K. Chesterton, *Orthodoxy* (London: Catholic Way Publishing, 2013), 108.

Contributors

Sarah Christmyer is a Catholic author, Bible teacher, and speaker with a special love for lectio divina and journaling as ways to draw closer to Christ in scripture. She is codeveloper of *The Great Adventure* Catholic Bible study program and author or coauthor of many of the studies. Sarah is an adjunct faculty member at St. Charles Borromeo Seminary in Philadelphia. She blogs at her website, www.ComeIntotheWord.com.

Kitty Cleveland is a wife, mother, and music missionary from New Orleans, Louisiana, who uses song and testimony to bring hope, healing, and encouragement to the faithful. She has released several CDs and has appeared numerous times on global Catholic television, on the radio, in concert, and as a keynote speaker throughout North America and Europe. For more information or to contact Kitty, see www.KittyCleveland.com.

Pat Gohn is an award-winning author, columnist, speaker, retreat leader, and host of the *Among Women* podcast. Pat holds a master's degree in theology. Her passion for faith formation and women's ministry led her to write her first book introducing the "feminine genius," *Blessed, Beautiful, and Bodacious: Celebrating the Gift of Catholic Womanhood*. Since then, more than two thousand women have enjoyed the retreat based on her book. Find out more at www.PatGohn.net.

As an international Pentecostal minister, **Barbara Heil** has traveled extensively, ministering in more than forty-five nations as a missionary, evangelist, and pastor. After an amazing journey she has found her way into the Catholic Church.

Barbara continues to be involved in a wide spectrum of Christian endeavor and to share the joy of the Gospel wherever she goes. Find Barbara at www.FromHisHeart.com.

Lisa M. Hendey is founder of *CatholicMom.com* and author of *The Grace of Yes* and the Chime Travelers fiction series for children. She employs media and her writing to share her passion for the New Evangelization. Lisa speaks internationally on faith, family, and technology, and travels worldwide to witness Catholic social teachings in action. Lisa and her husband, Greg, live in California and have two adult sons, Eric and Adam.

Stephanie Landsem writes novels that bring the unknown women of the Bible to life. The Living Water series—*The Well*, *The Thief*, and *The Tomb*—are biblically authentic stories of women who are transformed by encounters with Jesus. She lives in Minnesota with her husband and four children. You can find out more about Stephanie and her books at www.StephanieLandsem.com.

Laura Sobiech is a lifelong Catholic born and raised in Minnesota. She is the author of *Fly a Little Higher: How God Answered a Mom's Small Prayer in a Big Way*, a story about how God used her son Zach's suffering and death to bring grace into our world. She is a wife and mother of four. She spends much of her time sharing her family's story and advocating for childhood cancer research.

Teresa Tomeo is a motivational speaker, best-selling author, and the host of the daily morning show *Catholic Connection* on Ave Maria Radio. Teresa also cohosts the weekly EWTN-TV series *The Catholic View for Women*. Teresa has been featured on national news and talk shows discussing matters of faith, media awareness, and Catholic Church teachings especially as they relate to the culture and women.

Carol Younger teaches graduate courses in school psychology and counseling, and is active in adult faith formation in parishes. She is a senior fellow for the St. Paul Center for Biblical Theology. The author of *Retreat Companion for 33 Days to Morning Glory*, she presents at conferences and parishes on the unity of the Bible and the salvation story. The mother of three married children, she has seven grandchildren, a great-granddaughter, and a great-grandson on the way.

Kelly M. Wahlquist is a dynamic and inspiring Catholic author and speaker, and the founder of WINE: Women In the New Evangelization. She is the assistant director for the Archbishop Harry J. Flynn Catechetical Institute in the Archdiocese of St. Paul and Minneapolis.

Wahlquist is a contributor to *CatholicMom.com* and *Integrated Catholic Life*. She is the author of *Created to Relate: God's Design for Peace and Joy*. Wahlquist travels around the country speaking on the New Evangelization. She lives in Minnesota with her husband, Andy, and their three children.

Women IN *the* New Evangelization

As you read *Walk in Her Sandals*, you journeyed with Jesus in a very special way. While we hope it was a personal and prayerful experience from Palm Sunday to Pentecost, we also hope you sensed that it wasn't a solitary experience, not entirely anyway. The authors of this book and the fictional characters that came to life on these pages journeyed with you.

As you continue to journey through life, please know that you are never alone. There are women who are ready to walk with you right here, right now.

WINE: Women In the New Evangelization is a creative and inspired women's ministry that invigorates Catholic parishes through encouraging, supporting, and nurturing women in the faith and by equipping and mobilizing women as intentional disciples of Christ. WINE meets women where they are at on their journey and introduces them to relationship—relationship with Jesus Christ and relationships with other women. WINE empowers women to work within their God-given gifts as women to nurture, heal, and build up the Body of Christ.

WINE offers a variety of opportunities for women to minister to one another:

- Special events and conferences
- Unique women-centered book clubs
- Dynamic speaker series
- Uplifting articles and books
- Prayerful seasonal devotions
- A spiritual sisterhood that prays together and encourages one another

For more information about WINE, please visit CatholicVineyard.com.